STEAMPUNK MAGIC

Dear Spiritual Adventurer,

Congratulations on your choice to join the crew. As Captain of the airship, allow me to give you an idea of what you will be looking forward to in your years of service with us.

During your first year you will train with our more experienced crew members. You will receive a mentor who will guide you through the tools, spells, and rituals so necessary to Steampunk Magic. Your mentor will assist you in building or acquiring your tool kit—they can teach you to forge your own directional gear and help you procure your compass, rigging knife, and other vital magical tools. They will assist you in arranging your altar and teach you the invocations, salutes, and ceremonies unique to Steampunk Magic. At the end of your year-and-a-day training you will be afforded full membership into our ranks with all the rights and privileges of all the other members.

As you may have noticed on your first tour of the ship, there are numerous opportunities to advance in rank and skill. You may

choose to specialize in crafts, becoming one
of our Shipwrights or Artificers: engineers
and builders in the non Steampunk world.
Perhaps you'll outfit the entire crew with
a new set of goggles! Or instead you may
choose to cook and become an official Mess
Officer—preparing ritual tea cakes and
absinthe. Or perhaps you'll discover that
your skills with the compass are unsurpassed
and decide to become Navigator, charting
the course of our ship. It is even possible
to advance to Commander of our ship or, in
time, Captain of your own. As you can see,
with the right training, there is no limit
to what you may be able to do on board a
Steampunk Magic airship.

Throughout the duration of your stay, if
there are any questions that you have please
feel free to contact either myself or
any of the crew. We look forward to your
membership and I am certain your time with
us, as long or short as you may choose,
will be exciting, rewarding, and satisfying.
Again thank you and welcome aboard.

Gypsey Elaine Teague
Captain

Gypsey Elaine TEAGUE

STEAMPUNK MAGIC

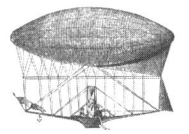

Working MAGIC Aboard the Airship

WEISERBOOKS
San Francisco, CA / Newburyport, MA

First published in 2013 by Red Wheel/Weiser
Red Wheel/Weiser, LLC
With offices at:
665 Third Street, Suite 400
San Francisco, CA 94107
www.redwheelweiser.com

Copyright © 2013 by Gypsey Elaine Teague

All rights reserved. No part of this publication may be reproduced or transmitted in any form or by any means, electronic or mechanical, including photocopying, recording, or by any information storage and retrieval system, without permission in writing from Red Wheel/Weiser, LLC. Reviewers may quote brief passages.

ISBN: 978-1-57863-539-9

Library of Congress Cataloging-in-Publication data available upon request

Cover design by Adrian Morgan
Interior by Deborah Dutton

Figure 1. Queen Victoria in 1887 photo courtesy of *storiesnow.com*

Printed in the United States of America
MAL
10 9 8 7 6 5 4 3 2 1

The paper used in this publication meets the minimum requirements of the American National Standard for Information Sciences—Permanence of Paper for Printed Library Materials Z39.48-1992 (R1997).

DEDICATION

This book would not be possible without Marla Roberson. She has been my mentor, inspiration, and wife for many years and shall continue to be for many more to come. When the idea of Steampunk Magic first came to me, it was Marla who talked me through the concept from "what if?" to "yes, this will work." It was during a fifteen-hour road trip in a Ford Escape from South Carolina to Dallas by way of Oklahoma that I explained, then expanded, and finally began to takes notes on what would eventually become this book and the system of Steampunk Magic.

Marla has been there through all the stages of writing: proofreading my work, commenting on my philosophies, and laughing at times as I tried to explain what was so easy at the end but so difficult at the beginning. This book is as much a product of her trust in me as it is an expanded concept of my vision. And for that I am eternally grateful. Marla, I love you.

This book is also in memory of Nora Stewart, whom we lost too soon. She supported this work and was very excited about joining us on the airship. Her energy pushes this work forward as a tribute to what she appreciated and a reminder that life is too short and we may lose it too easily.

CONTENTS

Prologue	1
1. What Is Steampunk Culture?	5
2. What Is Steampunk Magic?	19
3. The Airship and Crew	33
4. The Tools	47
5. Preparing the Altars and Casting the Circle	85
6. Rituals and Other Circles	107
7. Visioning and Divination	147
8. Spells	161
Conclusion	191
Epilogue	195
Resources	197
Index	209

To me a book is a message from the gods to mankind; or if not, it should never be published at all.
—Aleister Crowley

PROLOGUE

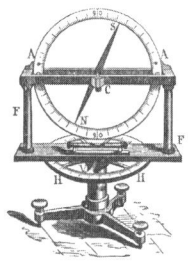

They start arriving around five o'clock in the evening. At six thirty a couple rings the bell on the porch of a renovated Victorian in a gentrified section of town and waits. She is wearing a long skirt with a bustle and lace neck blouse, and carrying a small clutch purse. On her head sits a top hat with a pair of brass goggles on the brim. Her hair falls from under the chapeau in tight curls. The gentleman leans on the carved wooden door casing. His long morning coat covers a crisp white shirt with pointed collars, a vest, pin-striped pants, and a shiny leather holster where a single action cap and ball pistol resides. He wears a bowler hat with matching goggles on the brim.

The host answers the door in work clothing and a stained leather apron. He has an old leather tool belt at his waist, and his face is slightly singed with what looks like soot. Goggles with very dark lenses hang from his neck, and his boots make a sharp clicking sound on the hardwood floors. As the old friends journey to the parlor, others are there—thirteen to be exact, since the two at the door were the last arrivals. The newcomers greet the others. All are dressed in some form of strange Victorian garb: many men and women are carrying elaborate firearms; most are wearing goggles, some very ornate; and three of the women are in tight corsets.

This could be the opening scene of a new Victorian movie or the first two paragraphs of a young adult novel; but these are real people, and they are part of a growing group of Steampunk Magicians.

At first glance steampunk and magic are not two subjects that are thought of as neighbors, or even friends. However, I realized a few years ago that magic has evolved so much in the past three generations that the skin that wraps our culture and path can be painted in a myriad of colors and styles. Because of this and the basic substance of steampunk I found that the two are indeed connective at many points along both continua.

Growing up I heard somewhere that magic was applied mathematics. Since I was never good at mathematics, I discounted the chance of ever being good at magic. I didn't understand at that time (I was six years old) that applied mathematics in this case was actually just doing the same thing (a + b + c = d) over and over again with the same results. Again, it didn't matter what the process looked like, as long as the process was identical each time.

Now, as an elder and high priestess, I do indeed understand and teach my students that although the nomenclature of Steampunk Magic might differ from what they are used to, that doesn't make it any more or less effective or "real." With that clarity I began the synthesis of melding steampunk and magic into a practical method of processes and effects for the Victorian futurists. I have hosted a steampunk conference in South Carolina, written on the subject, appeared in books on the style and fashion of the genre, and studied how this all may be applied to the magical path that I follow. This book is the result of my efforts.

This volume is a beginning text. It is not meant to be the be-all and end-all of Steampunk Magic, nor is it meant to be kept secret from the world. This introduction is simply that—a starting place meant to be used, modified, and expanded upon as its spells and potions are finessed. I only ask that you keep copious notes to be passed on to the next generation of magical historical futurists.

1
WHAT IS STEAMPUNK CULTURE?

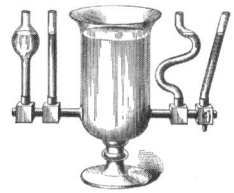

"Would you like to see the Time Machine itself?" asked the Time Traveler. And therewith, taking the lamp in his hand, he led the way down the long, draughty corridor to his laboratory. I remember vividly the flickering light, his queer, broad head in silhouette, the dance of the shadows, how we all followed him, puzzled but incredulous, and how there in the laboratory we beheld a larger edition of the little mechanism which we had seen vanish from before our eyes. Parts were of nickel, parts of ivory, parts had certainly been filed or sawn out of rock crystal. The thing was generally complete, but the twisted crystalline bars lay unfinished upon the bench beside some sheets of drawings, and I took one up for a better look at it. Quartz it seemed to be.

—H. G. Wells, *The Time Machine*

Ladies and Gentlemen, boys and girls of all ages, let me take you to a world of steam and brass, guns and goggles, where electricity never caught on and if you fly it's with helium and hydrogen in large airships. A world where there is fog and smog and smoke and flame. A world of war and peace, and bustles—from the city and the ladies. Where Victoria is Queen, and the sun never sets on the British Empire. Ladies and gentlemen, allow me to offer you a world of steampunk.

In steampunk, the brass is shinier, the guns are deadlier, the women are prettier, and the men are more muscular. Everything is bigger and sharper and cuter and edgier while being reserved, genteel, and holding to nineteenth-century morals and ethics. Men tip their hats and hold doors for ladies. Ladies bow in long skirts and corsets.

Before I discuss the path of Steampunk Magic, let me try to explain exactly what I mean by "steampunk." Steampunk is the juxtaposition of nineteenth-century science fiction and twenty-first-century reality; or, put more simply, it can be thought of as Victorian science fiction grown up, a futuristic Victoriana, where anything is possible as long as you don't use too much electricity, gas, diesel, or atomic power.

Steampunk is . . . a futuristic Victoriana, where anything is possible as long as you don't use too much electricity, gas, diesel, or atomic power.

Steampunk takes the works of Jules Verne, H. G. Wells, and other science fiction writers of the Victorian era and transports them to our time—or at least a time that could have been, if steam had remained the primary power source. Steampunk is a Victorian "what if." And there lies the rub, as they say. There is no real definition

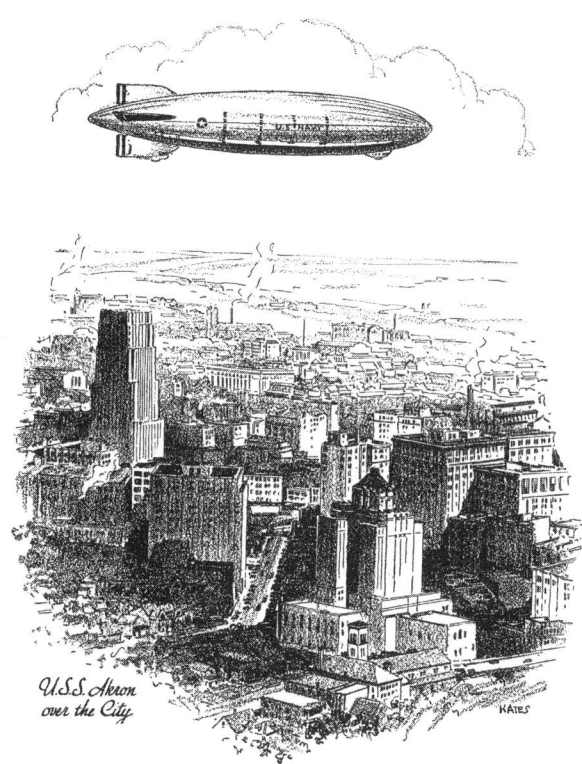

of what steampunk is or can be, since there is no limit to the number of alternate histories that could have evolved from the time of Victoria.

When Herbert George Wells wrote *The Time Machine* in 1895, his genre was termed "scientific fiction." At that time the future was a wild and wonderful place to long for. It was a future with no war, famine, pestilence, fear, or poverty. There would be unlimited travel by submersible, airship, and fast train and carriage. The world would be what they had promised it was going to be—instead of the tawdry, lousy, fouled up mess that the Victorian populace of England and America were all too familiar with.

What Is Steampunk Culture?

Add to the historic works of H. G. Wells the undersea submersible of Nemo in Jules Verne's *Twenty Thousand Leagues Under the Sea*, Mary Shelley's *Frankenstein,* and finally stir in the architecture of the Victorian age, and you have a breeding ground for a future not quite realized but possibly attainable.

Now, more than one hundred years later, some of us long to return to this time of steam, brass, copper, and gas. We forget the short life expectancies of that time, the filthy living con-

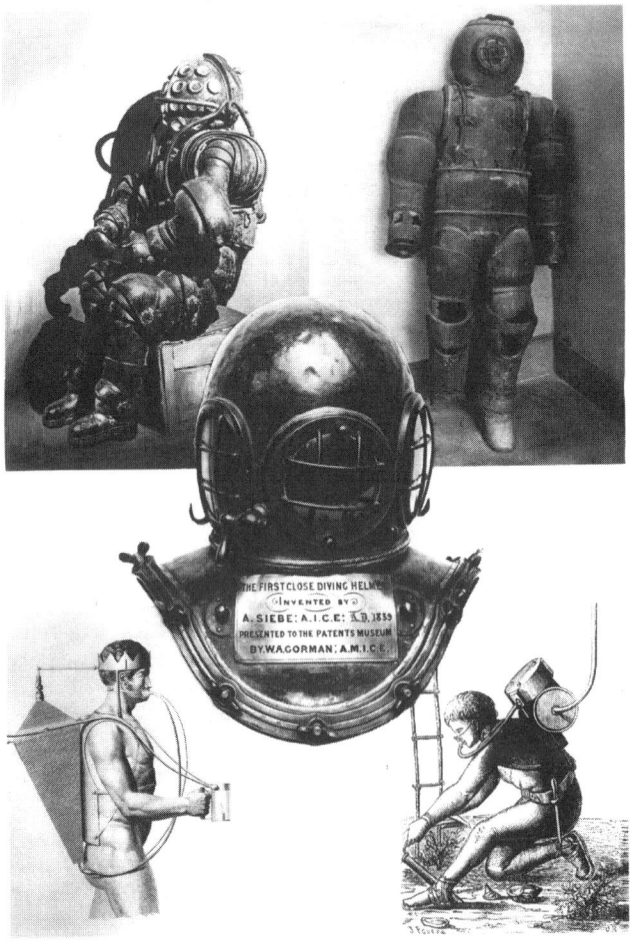

ditions, and the deplorable sanitation of the early Victorian era. We would be appalled at the medical and technological backwardness as compared to our hospitals and digital world. But hindsight is always filtered from reality, and the steampunk genre has become the new and more cleaned up, pressed, and polished history of the world. It is a genre that spans art and science to include everything from computers to books, hardware to fashion.

The Beginning of Steampunk

It all started in the 1980s. At that time a subculture of science fiction found a foothold in literature and science fiction conventions. These paths-not-taken alternative histories spurred on by the goth followers became a new mini-genre to follow. K. W. Jeter, an American science fiction and horror writer, first coined the phrase "steampunk" in April, 1987, as a way to identify what he and others of his time were writing. With books such as *Infernal Devices, Morlock Night,* and the seminal work *The Difference Engine* by William Gibson and Bruce Sterling, steampunk burst onto the horizon of those who enjoyed the different, the alternative, or the dystopic. Very slowly at first readers of these works took them to heart and began asking, and then demanding, more. The costumes came next; pieces from thrift stores and other remnant houses, and original Victorian hand-me-downs found in chests and trunks in attics. By the turn of this century,

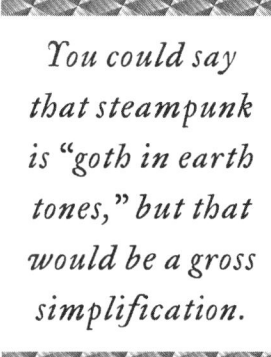

You could say that steampunk is "goth in earth tones," but that would be a gross simplification.

What Is Steampunk Culture? 9

and one hundred years after the death of Victoria, the fans of steampunk were spreading everywhere.

Another definition of steampunk is "what goth grew up to be." This is a limited definition and not completely accurate, but it does touch on the history of the movement. The goth trend of the 1980s seems to have many tenets of the steampunk movement of the 1990s and 2000s, but it is neither completely accurate nor applicable. Steampunk is a genre that is many things to many people. While the goths wore dark clothing, darker hair, and even darker attitudes, espousing a neo-Victorian appearance of a bleak postpunk genre, the cyberpunk movement (a subgroup of the goths) incorporated the high-tech future of movies such as *Blade Runner* and *The Matrix*. You could say that steampunk is "goth in earth tones," but that would be a gross simplification.

Steampunk is the DIY subculture of anything that has to do with steam.

One of the things making "steampunk" a difficult work to define is the word "punk." Many in the mainstream, whatever the mainstream may be, think of punk in a pejorative view and associate punks with punk rock or the anti-establishment of the early goth movement. However, it is important to remember that the term punk refers to a do-it-yourself attitude, and

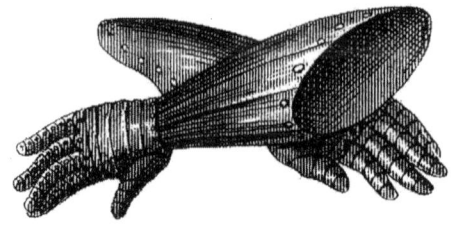

Steampunk Magic

punks are a subculture of a larger group. So, punk rock would be a subculture of rock music; cyberpunk is a subculture of the technological mainstream; and steampunk is the DIY subculture of anything that has to do with steam.

Steampunk Today

In March, 2010, the Library of Congress created a subject heading for Steampunk. Up until that time you had to forage through Alternative Histories or Speculative Fictions to find what you were looking for. This is a great leap in the realm of steampunk, because now the genre has gained acceptance in the field with a standardized vocabulary, subjects, and keywords. In the March 4, 2010 issue of *Library Journal,* John Klima published a list of classic and new core titles for the genre. Nick Gevers' *Extraordinary Engines: The Definitive Steampunk Anthology* is a fine collection of short stories that revolve around the alternative history of steam. A novel I'd recommend for young adults is Scott Westerfeld's *Leviathan.* There are a few hundred-plus steampunk novels and anthologies currently available, and they run the gamut of very fine to very poor. See the Resources section in the back of this book for a list of more steampunk books.

Steampunk Magazine (www.steampunkmagazine.com) showcases the work of budding artists, authors, and inventors. The magazine is free to the public, although they do ask for donations if possible, and they sell paper copies for a subscription rate. The magazine has only been in production since October of 2009, but it presents a professional product and seems to be very popular. I've seen it sold and traded at many conventions such as Dragon*Con and The Steampunk Exhibition Ball.

Not to be outdone by graphic novels and journals, Antarctic Press has released *Steampunk Palin,* a less-than-politically-correct comic about Sarah Palin, John McCain, and Barack Obama fighting the forces of Big Oil and Nuke led by Al Gore. Ben Dunn, the illustrator, dresses Palin in the typical bodice and accessories so favored by steampunk fans, while Jim Felkner writes great one-liners for Palin to deliver as she saves the planet.

Steampunk's influence can be seen on the big and small screens as well. Movies are often the escape of the masses, as well as a window to the world of the future. Even though the time period is early Victorian, the movie remake of the popular television show *Wild Wild West* (1999) has excellent steampunk gimmicks, such as the flying bicycle of Artemis Gordon, and the steam-powered wheelchair and giant spider of Dr. Loveless. Other examples include: *The League of Extraordinary Gentlemen,* the BBC 2010 and American 2012 Sherlock Holmes movies, *Van Helsing,* and the flying airships of *The Mummy Returns* and *The Golden Compass.* All have the requisite ma-

chines and contraptions that are so popular with the new movement of steam over nuclear and electricity.

As I write this, I'm listening to one of the better steampunk bands of the moment. The group is called Abney Park, and they're from the Seattle area. This group not only uses industrial sounds such as airship engines and propellers in their soundtracks, but they have their entire band outfitted in steampunk clothing and retrofitted instruments. Although at times their lyrics are hard to understand, their music is not. It's haunting at times and hard-driving at others. Many of Abney Park's songs, such as "Airship Pirates" and "Herr Drosselmeyer's Doll," revolve around the motifs of robotics with gears and flying airships—both popular subjects in steampunk literature. What makes Abney Park somewhat unique

> *There are four main tenets you can use to identify someone who is in a steampunk persona or costume: goggles, corsets (or vests), hats, and guns.*

is their take on the retrofitting of their instruments. They use a lot of industrial copper, brass, and Tesla-like special effects during their videos and live performances. For a list of other steampunk bands playing today, see the Resources section.

For a number of years I have been involved in steampunk as a hobby and getaway. It started at Dragon*Con, the largest science fiction and fantasy convention in the Southeast, held each year over Labor Day weekend in Atlanta. In 2011, Dragon*Con had a self-reported attendance of more than 52,000 people. There among the many Star Trek, Star Wars, Firefly, and comic book characters were a growing number of men and women in hats, goggles, and corsets, some carrying guns. These participants were young, old, male, female, married, single, and all the other permutations that make up society.

When I first saw them, I thought, what an odd assortment of characters. I didn't see the connection to the genre of literature and originally thought that they were a troupe of actors and actresses preparing for some special role. As a performer myself (I was a member of the Society of Creative

Anachronism for many years), I appreciated the costuming and the craftsmanship it took to sew, glue, screw, and fabricate their elaborate pieces.

Although conventions such as Dragon*Con and others are generalist conventions, meaning they cater to all forms of science fiction, fantasy, and gaming, other conventions are specifically targeted to the steampunk aficionado. Upstate Steampunk, held in Greenville/Anderson, South Carolina, is a perfect example of a targeted convention that will gather fans from all over the Southeast for a weekend of all things steam. While at generalist conventions you may see a few steampunk venders and programs, at this ball you will see exclusively steampunk interests represented. This is an excellent example of how popular the movement has become.

Finally, we come to the center of all of this. There must be a plan or architecture to the story, right? Without the architecture of a new history or the art to envision it, there would only be literature; and although that is still the original medium for entertainment it is more effective in the three dimensional world to have toys and tools. Because of this even computers and other electronic devices now so essential to our world have become a favorite for steampunk creationists. Keyboards are retrofitted with antique typewriter keys and mounted in heavy brass and exotic woods. Computer towers are outfitted with gauges, pipes, and gears protruding from all sides of the machine. Even the lowly mouse and thumb drive are made to look historically futuristic.

Steampunk design is artful, and it's the little touches that make it so much fun. There are steampunk bathtubs, watch gear jewelry, and mainstream clothiers that are designing for individuals and the home that they live in. There is a myriad of options for steampunk costumes, from the ornate to the bizarre. Basically, if it is Victorian, then most will accept the fashion as a form of steampunk.

I contend that there are four main tenets you can use to identify someone who is in a steampunk persona or costume: goggles, corsets (or vests), hats, and guns.

The first is some form of goggles. The goggles don't have to be functional, and in fact the more fanciful and augmented they are, the more they are admired. Some goggles even have removable lenses and may be fitted with standard round lenses from optometrists.

The second indicators are corsets or vests. These are not necessarily the tight-fitting Victorian wasp waist corsets of the period, but they are waist adornments nonetheless. They may be waist cinchers or another piece of clothing that approximates the look of corsets of the time. It is interesting to note that men also use a waist covering. Many of the steampunk men wear buttoned vests.

Third are hats. There are hats for all occasions: top, bowler, wide or narrow brim, Cowboy Stetson, with feathers, without, leather, and some are even miniature. They are prevalent everywhere at conventions and gatherings. Hats are also used to hold the goggles on the brim, although many build elaborate hats that support entire fantasy structures.

Finally, there are guns. While many steampunk folks collect or wear real antique guns, most carry the most exotic built pistols and rifles ever seen. There are some guns so large that they have built-in straps to carry them. Others are motorized with smoke emitters for authenticity.

Oftentimes steampunks will make their own costumes. One class offered at Dragon*Con as part of the Alternate History track covered making fantasy weapons as well as weapons that were period during the time. Another class on the Costuming track discussed how to make corsets, distress denim, and put together a complete steampunk look. Many of these classes ran through the night and into the very early morning hours and were standing room only.

Steampunk has become more than a hobby to some and less than a lifestyle to others. I was at Dragon*Con in September, and every time I would pass someone who was in some form of steampunk garb we would nod knowingly to each other, very much as when I had an MG sports car and I would flash my lights when I saw another MG. It is a club that we are all members of, without dues or rules. We enjoy the uniqueness of our clothing, tools, and accoutrements without being flashy or secretive. Ask anyone in Steampunk garb about their costume and they will gladly spend hours talking with you about where and how they came up with each piece. It is the all-inclusive nature of the genre.

2

WHAT IS STEAMPUNK MAGIC?

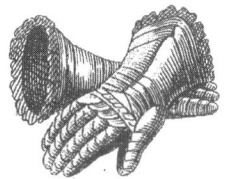

Indubitably, Magick is one of the subtlest and most difficult of the sciences and arts. There is more opportunity for errors of comprehension, judgment and practice than in any other branch of physics.
—ALEISTER CROWLEY, *THE CONFESSIONS OF ALEISTER CROWLEY*

So, why steampunk magic? Why not? Perhaps we wish history were different, because so much of it was actually very grim, and we want to remember the glamorous and romantic parts. Steampunk gives us the opportunity to take the best and dump the rest. We all want the future to be better, and we all have a unique approach to what we see for the future. In Steampunk Magic the aether that we sail through, work in, and peer beyond allows us the power to perceive what is before us, unobstructed by the filters and layers of twenty-first century doubt and questioning.

How Is Steampunk Magic Different from Other Systems of Magic?

I believe that in Steampunk Magic the visions are more accurate. The spells are more concentrated and directed to the task at hand. Even though you may, and I say *may* with trepidation, perform magic naked with an index finger, in Steampunk Magic the tools enhance the magic and therefore the result.

In the very earliest pre-recorded history, the magicians, mages, and wise men and women looked around at their surroundings and worked with what was at hand. Herbs, seasons, tides, animals, and the cycles of the crops were known to these elders, and with that knowledge the community prospered.

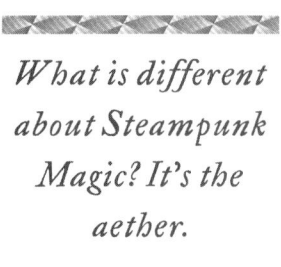

What is different about Steampunk Magic? It's the aether.

In a way, Steampunk Magic isn't so different from many other magical traditions and paths that have retained what is successful over the years and eliminated what was not: we look at what works, we write those spells and procedures in our grimoires, and we keep experimenting. Magic works because the process employed works.

Many of us have become complacent in our application to magic and therefore lost much of the connection to what worked for us, and, most importantly, what was familiar. We read a book that we purchase at the airport and that makes up the bulk of our knowledge of twenty-first-century magic. We expect, or hope, that if we read the book enough, we will glean something useful that will work for us. In reality, though, we don't understand what the author is trying to convey since we aren't familiar with the principles of the path. Without a point of reference, the book becomes a sale item at a yard sale; then we buy another book, hoping that this time things will be different.

In any magic system you must start with the basics that you recognize. If you are a woman who follows an earth-based path, it is unrealistic to expect you to understand and follow a masculine Norse-based tradition. Your points of reference are not there. It's the same with Steampunk Magic. Although this system will work for anyone, those who are already familiar with steampunk and magic will quickly grasp the concepts of this new style of magic and grok the meanings more easily.

The Aether

What is different about this system of magic? The answer is simple yet quite complex: it's the aether. In ancient times the aether was considered the material above our planet and the other planets and bodies of space. It was the clear air that the gods breathed in their celestial palaces, and mortal men and women aspired to breathe it to be more godlike.

The Greeks took this idea to such a level that they created a deity for the substance. In the first century BC, Latin author Gaius Julius Hyginus wrote in Fabulae that Aether was the child of Chaos. Further, and this is the connection that ties

Aether to our world and our traditions, Alcman writes in his fifth surviving fragment from the Scholia that Aether was the father of Gaia, the mother of us all.

Icarus and Daedalus flew high into the heavens to escape their captivity, and man has always aspired to escape the confines of the Earth as the gods. On November 21, 1783, Jean-François Pilâtre de Rozier and François Laurent d'Arlandes flew the first hot air balloon in France after petitioning King Louis XVI for the honor. In December, 1903, at that now famous beach off Kitty Hawk, North Carolina, the Wright brothers from Ohio flew the first heavier-than-air craft, proving again that man's desire to gain the aether knew no limits. On April 12, 1961, the Soviet cosmonaut Yuri Gagarin flew the first manned spacecraft to escape the Earth's atmosphere and actually fly into the aether. All these accomplishments were considered magical in either nature or practicality at the time; and each example brought us closer to our gods.

According to Aristotle the aether was devoid of all properties. It was neither hot nor cold, wet nor dry. The aether given to us by the philosophers and alchemists existed but could not be proven by any of the senses. We cannot see it, taste it, touch

Steampunk Magic

it, feel it, or prove that it surrounds us in our daily lives. However, even if we cannot experience something in the physical sense it does not mean that we cannot experience that property in the ethereal or non-physical sense. Just as gravity exists, though we cannot experience it with any of our senses, the aether is all around us; and we must learn to harness that which is without by the powers within.

Our airships fly through this aether, surrounding us with the essences and inspiration of the gods. And as we get closer to our gods, we hope to derive wisdom and knowledge in the process. Therefore we go ever higher and farther, searching for our definition of the Divine.

Although Steampunk Magic is practical in all settings of magical work, it is specifically useful for *visioning and divination*. The aether is everywhere, and with the use of the aether the magician may see what is sought, discover what is hidden, and formulate what is required. The Steampunk Magician has the tools that many other systems do not and the aether that many other systems only give a cursory reference to. The Steampunk Magician flies high and deep into the aether and returns better for the experience.

Steampunk Magic gives the practitioner the specific tools and rituals to enter the aether, contact the gods and spirits within, and perceive what is there. It is grounded in historic traditions that are designed to harness the energies of the aether for the betterment of the airship and its

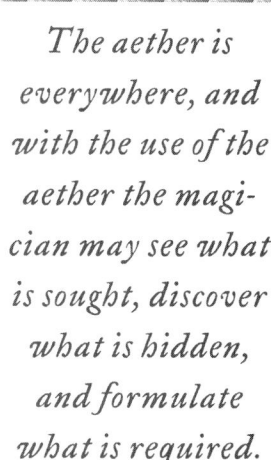

The aether is everywhere, and with the use of the aether the magician may see what is sought, discover what is hidden, and formulate what is required.

members, and to succeed where other systems may have failed. For example, in circle and spell work, the adventurer penetrates the aether, and with goggles, compass, and lamp, all questions may be answered and all needs may be achieved.

Gods, Spirits, and Notables in Steampunk Magic

There are no specific gods or sprits in Steampunk Magic, though if there were to be one, truth be told, it would probably be She who began it all by ascending the throne: Victoria. But Steampunk Magic is a system of procedures that do not revolve around or depend upon a specific deity, and anyone can practice it, whether they are pagan or not. This allows the system to be attuned to the individual in a way that few if any other systems allow. All deities are welcomed in our system, and all deities are invoked, depending on your individual religious path.

> *There are no specific gods or sprits in Steampunk Magic, though if there were to be one, it would probably be She who began it all by ascending the throne: Victoria.*

Here are a few of the notable individuals who have contributed their knowledge, wisdom, or existence to the era and the fabric of the time.

Queen Victoria

The first and foremost notable in all steampunk history must be Victoria, Queen of the United Kingdom of Great Britain,

Ireland, and Empress of India. Victoria was born May 24, 1819, ascended the throne on June 20, 1837, and passed away on January 22, 1901. During her reign England and the world achieved an unparalleled level of industrial accomplishment. It was during this time that many of the industrial inventors, writers, philosophers, and historians made their mark on the world, not only in the British Isles but in the Americas as well.

Figure 1. Queen Victoria in 1887.

During the Victorian Era the population of England more than doubled due to increased birthrates in the British Isles and a decrease in the early mortality of the population. There were no major famines, plagues, or great catastrophes other than the Great Famine in Ireland early in Queen Victoria's reign. Sewage disposal was introduced during this time, and the medical community, though still rather barbaric, made great strides ahead of where it had been during the Renaissance or the Middle Ages.

At this time the educational standards of the country also improved. In 1870 British state education became mandatory for every child under the age of ten, increasing the literacy of the country. This led to a smarter country, and a more productive one with the next generation. Lights were improved with the gas mantle, similar to today's gas camping lights, and streets were better lit, so crime slowed slightly. Workers were also able to work longer hours under artificial light, so factories were kept running throughout the night, increasing production that was shipped on the new rail lines.

In Europe you had H. G. Wells, Jules Verne, Lewis Carroll, Charles Dickens, the Bronte sisters, and William Makepeace Thackeray. Across the pond, Harriet Beecher Stowe, Ralph Waldo Emerson, Nathaniel Hawthorne, Herman Melville,

Mark Twain, Walt Whitman, and Henry David Thoreau were making their mark on the literary landscape. Every one of these authors donated something to the times and to steampunk, but the two who are most thought of as steampunk authors are H. G. Wells and Jules Verne.

H. G. Wells

As an author and historic prophet, Herbert George (H. G.) Wells shines above all others save Jules Verne, whom most consider his equal. Born in England in 1866, his writings came late in the Victorian period. *The Time Machine* wasn't published until 1895—just six years before the Victorian era was to end. However, the lasting effect of Wells' fiction was to forever impact the world.

Wells' life was as turbulent as his writings, or the other way around, and he was a social commentator through his scientific fiction and nonfiction until his death. Wells was an early advocate of polyamory and had four children: two sons with his wife Lynn, and a son and daughter with other liaisons he enjoyed and his wife approved of. Although the term polyamory wasn't around in Victorian times, the concept existed, and his dalliances, as noted in Andrea Lynn's *Shadow Lovers: The Last*

Affairs of H. G. Wells, were well known to his wife and inner circle of friends. His personal life notwithstanding, he is lauded as one of the fathers of steampunk and must be remembered as such.

Jules Verne

The other grandmaster of steampunk, Jules Verne is probably best known for the Nautilus and Captain Nemo in *Twenty Thousand Leagues Under the* Sea with *War of the Worlds* coming in a close second. As far as classic steampunk novels go, I personally believe that *Twenty Thousand Leagues Under the Sea* is the epitome of steampunk work of that time.

    Verne was borne in France in 1828 and married late in life to a widow with two daughters. They later had a son together. His family life was satisfactory until he was shot by his nephew while returning home one day. The first shot missed him, but the second shot struck Verne in the leg, and he limped for the rest of his life. The incident was never made public, and the nephew was sent away to an asylum out of reach of the press. This injury may have precipitated Verne's death, but there is no evidence to prove that supposition. Toward the end of his life

Verne's writings turned more somber, and by the time of his passing in 1905 he was more or less a dystopian writer.

Edgar Allan Poe

Edgar Allan Poe was writing early in the Victorian Era. Many people I talk to about steampunk literature say it's a shame that Poe missed the cutoff to be considered a steampunk author, but I think he qualifies. Poe may have died during the early years of Victoria (he passed in 1849), but the fact remains that Poe does indeed fit the time frame and location of the Victorian era.

It is also interesting that both sides of the Mason–Dixon Line claim Poe as one of their own, and it seems perhaps to keep the two sides at bay he died somewhere in the middle. Poe was born in Boston and was orphaned early on. John and Frances Allen adopted Poe and moved him to Richmond, Virginia. When he was just forty years old Poe died in Baltimore, Maryland from any of a number of diseases and causes. Some say tuberculosis, alcohol, drugs, cholera, suicide, stroke, or even rabies. The final reason will be one of conjecture. Maybe for someone as morose and dark as Poe that's the way he would have wanted to be remembered.

> *The three most noted authors of the Victorian era were troubled, conflicted men.*

Whatever caused his death, Poe's life was one of triumph at times for his writing. He is credited with inventing the gothic genre and the sub-class American gothic. He was the master of the macabre and the father, or grandfather, if you will, of gothic horror masters H. P. Lovecraft and Stephen King. Poe was also instrumental in the early adoption and acceptance of scientific fiction with such works as *The Balloon-Hoax* and *The Narrative of Arthur Gordon Pym of Nantucket.* In the end he will be remembered for his writing as much as the odd circumstances of his death.

Similar to Wells and Verne, Poe was ahead of his time and died with children both within and without his marriage. The three most noted authors of the Victorian era were troubled, conflicted men who wrote as they saw the world, which was not the happy and carefree world we see in later fiction.

Nikola Tesla

Tesla was born in the village of Smiljan in the Serbian state of Austria. He immigrated to the United States in 1891 and became one of the proponents of alternating current. Although alternating current is not considered steampunk, Tesla's use of the aether to transmit power puts him in the forefront of technical Steampunk Magicians.

> *Tesla's use of the aether to transmit power puts him in the forefront of technical Steampunk Magicians.*

During much of his life, Tesla experienced visions preceded by a blinding light. (We now believe these occurrences may have been due to a neurological condition or a type of migraine.) What would ensue was an idea or design that was fully formed and ready for construction. Tesla seldom drew or sketched any of his creations; rather, he began construction from the schematics he saw in his vision and proceeded from there.

Mary Shelley

Mary Shelley died during the Victorian time; however, many may say that she is not a Victorian author. I contend that she was a Steampunk author without being a purely Victorian one. When Shelley wrote *The Modern Prometheus,* better known today as *Frankenstein,* Shelley was just twenty-two years old. She was also of the mind that "do it yourself" was more than a phrase to be used later. Victor Frankenstein was one of the most prominent and original do-it-yourselfers. Here is a man who took parts from others to create a unique life, albeit his version of it.

A close examination of *Frankenstein* shows the depths of knowledge that Shelley had of the laboratory and the creative process. While current steampunks do not attempt to create life, they do attempt to create something original from a pile of discards or used items. This is the ultimate creativity of the movement of steampunk and what Shelley conveyed in her novel. When I think of a steampunk heroine in literature, I draw inspiration from Shelley and her originality for creating something from something else.

※

Victoria was the last monarch who claimed the House of Hanover. With her death and the ascension of Edward VII, the British crown became the House of Saxe-Coburg and Gotha, ending both a movement yet to be created and a great House never again to return.

3

THE AIRSHIP AND CREW

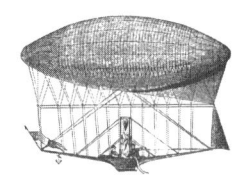

The machine does not isolate man from the great problems of nature but plunges him more deeply into them.
—Antoine de Saint-Exupery

In Steampunk Magic, instead of having a coven you have a ship—an airship. In this chapter, we'll talk about the metaphor of the airship as it applies to both Steampunk Magic and the counterparts of traditional paths.

The Airship

Generally there are thirteen members in a coven, with one designated as the high priest or priestess. A coven may have a high priest or priestess, or both. Like most covens, the airship of Steampunk Magic has a name and members (here the members are called a crew). Each crew member has a function, even if it's only temporary. The model for the crew is roughly taken from the Victorian naval model of the day. The officers are senior members of the crew and have practiced Steampunk Magic the longest. They understand what it takes to perform the necessary spells and rituals. They are also the teachers and the writers of the craft. They are our elders in the system, and we look to them for guidance and leadership.

Four Basic Steampunk Styles

First, let's discuss what an airship crew might look like. In *The Steampunk Bible,* Jeff Vandermeer proposes that there are four basic styles, or even personality types, of steampunk dress: Street Urchins, Tinkerers, Explorers, and Aesthetes. His proposition is relatively accurate in relation to Steampunk Magic.

The Street Urchin

In steampunk you see many younger or newer members of the genre dressed in DIY clothing that is built on the cheap from household items and inexpensive pieces found at thrift shops. It is a mish-mash of styles and decades in and around the Victorian period, and no one cares if the outfit is 100 percent authentic, because steampunk is a DIY genre that lends itself to these folks perfectly. Many beginners to Steampunk Magic start as the Street Urchins. They find their way to the airships by word of mouth, or a friend brings them, and they outfit themselves as best they can so as to not stand out in mundane jeans and T-shirts. Many of the newest members of your airship will be Street Urchins by default until they either choose to remain as such or find a persona they like better.

There are four personality types of steampunk dress.

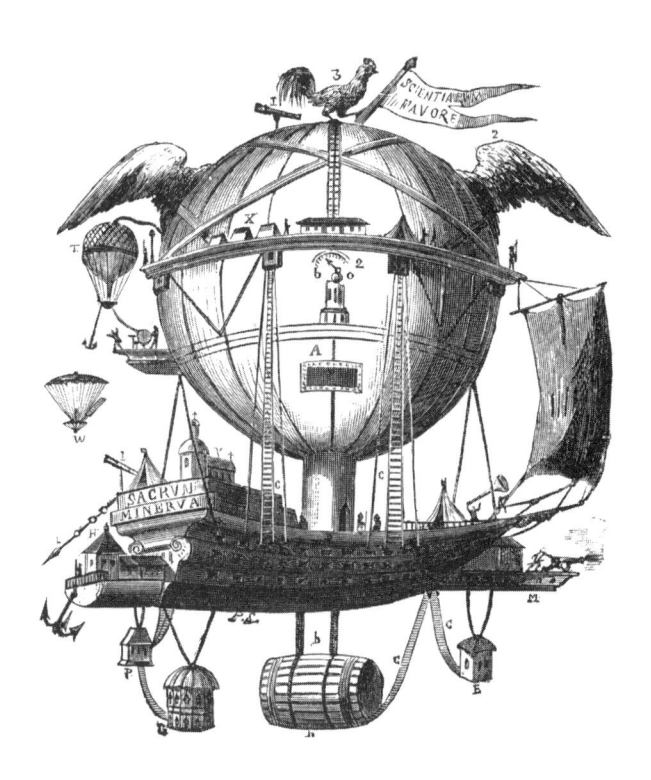

The Tinkerer

The Tinkerer is the worker and the inventor. These folks will look at something and see what it can be in its new life. Their ships are outfitted well with retro technology to enhance ritual, and as such they will be at the forefront of new spells, ceremonies, and tools on the altar. They are the ones who spend their spare time experimenting with anything they can find. You'll find them at the local hardware store, and if you ask what they're doing there they'll tell you they won't know what they are looking for until they see it. Tinkerers are able to dress in the heaviest clothing—soot covered, wrinkled, and with tools in hand—and still be presentable. I think of myself as a Tinkerer.

I have a friend at our local building center who no longer asks if she can help me. Instead she asks me what I'm working on. It makes the search much easier and more productive.

The Explorer

The Explorer wants to find the next new world. Though much of their travels and explorations are metaphoric, they are nonetheless the adventurers who look ahead and wonder what's out there. On an airship the explorers are oftentimes the navigators, and they chart the path of the ship. This means they are responsible for planning the ritual and setting up what is necessary to perform it either as a closed circle or a public display. Their garb is often safari shorts or long cargo-type pants. They wear high boots, canvas belts, and pith helmets with goggles on the brim. There are many accessories that they can carry, such as a compass, lamps, and armaments to repel unwanted animals (or humans). Explorers claim to have the most fun because they are always looking to adorn their costumes with more brass and bronze.

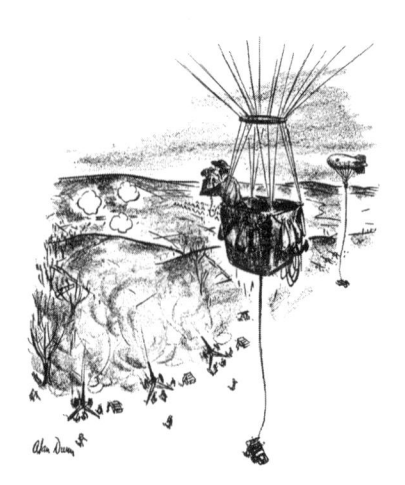

The Aesthete

The Aesthete is the photo op of the convention, and in the airship they are often the High Priest or Priestess. These are the bon vivants; often when we think of steampunk, these are the folks who come to mind. They take fashion and grooming to an entirely new level and have a hat, shoes, and corset or vest for every occasion. This is not to say that they are insincere, narcissistic, or elitist—they are just well-groomed and fashionable. They can be counted on to have the most recent offering from commercial clothing companies or perhaps their own sewing abilities. I have a very good friend who thinks nothing of spending countless hours gluing crystals onto a set of tails in intricate gear patterns for a convention. He is the ultimate dresser and an incredible milliner, and we always look forward to what he designs for himself and those around him.

These four types of steampunkers are generalizations. As with this cross-section of humanity, we are all different, and therefore our garb and dress are different, too. You may find yourself identifying with each of these four classifications at different times of the week or the month. We all have a tinkerer in us. We are all adventurers and explorers. And I hazard to say that we have all overdressed at times and underdressed at others in our day-to-day lives. Let's see how these general types fit into the specific roles of the airship crew members.

The Crew

The Captain and the Commander

The Captain and the Commander are the most experienced elders of the airship. They provide leadership to the group, often scheduling the rituals, planning the teaching of the new crew members, helping with garb and tools, and inspiring those who are uncertain as to whether Steampunk Magic is for them. Both the Captain and the Commander may perform rituals and other duties as the situation requires.

> *The Captain and the Commander are the most experienced elders of the airship.*

The Captain is usually the most experienced member of the ship, and the one with the longevity in the system. There are times when the Commander, as second in command, may step in as acting Captain, such as: when the Captain is absent, when the particular specialty of a ritual is one that the Commander has a better grasp on, or when the Commander requests it.

When I use the term "Captain" I am referring to the officiating officer for a specific ritual. There are a few rare cases where both the Captain and Commander have roles in the same ritual, but usually it is just the Captain. It is also important to remember that, as in any group, depending on the needs or desires of the ship, other senior individuals may perform the rituals. At any time whoever is performing the ritual is in the Captain's position and is referred to as the Captain.

The Captain and the Commander represent the airship in public and are the points of contact with other covens or airships. Their attire is often very ornate, with creases and dress accessories. The airship's key is often either hung from a chain around the Captain's neck or kept on a chain in his vest or her corset.

When I use the term "Captain" I am referring to the officiating officer for a specific ritual.

The Artificer

The Artificer is the construction engineer who builds or repairs the magical tools of the ship. They are responsible for maintaining the altar and keeping the magical equipment. With help from the Shipwright, they set up the altar before the ceremony and at the conclusion of the ceremony they take the altar down and store it away. They are also responsible for the administrative construction of the circle. In our case, we have a box for our tools, and our altar cloth folds to be portable and to fit whatever table is used.

The Artificer's clothing is usually utilitarian in nature and may include a belt of tools worn on the waist or slung as a bandolier. Their style could be classified as the Tinkerer.

The Shipwright

The Shipwright is the builder and designer. They are responsible for the physical space of the circle and keeping the lights going. With the Artificer, the Shipwright is present at the beginning and ending of a ritual to set up and take down all the altars. The Shipwright reports to the Artificer when the circle is ready to populate the altars, and states this as part of their opening ritual before the circle begins.

The Shipwright is often dressed in worker garb. Since they are, similar to the Artificer, in a construction/maintenance mode they are expected to be ready to get dirty if necessary before, during, or after ritual. Heavy fabrics and long sleeves are often seen as garb for the Shipwright. Their tools are larger pieces of equipment and seldom make it into the circle; however, the maintenance tools are never too far away.

The Purser

The next member of the crew is the Purser. This individual is responsible for the monies of the ship. When supplies are needed such as candles, coal, ritual food, and potluck dinners, the Purser acquires supplies by collecting donations from the crew.

Because the work of a Purser does not involve dirt or grime, they are often dressed in a white shirt or blouse with fancy cuffs and jewelry. In Victorian times the Purser was often from a well-to-do family and well educated. Their ability was highly prized, and they were expected to stay clean and undisturbed in their garb. The dress of the Purser may be one of the Aesthete or the Explorer.

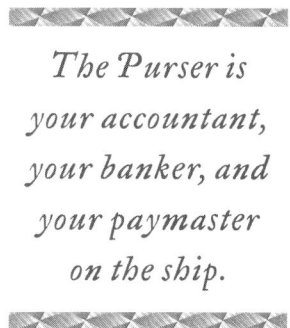

The Purser is your accountant, your banker, and your paymaster on the ship.

The Mess Officer

While on the subject of food, there is the Mess Officer. He or she may be referred to as the cook, although that would be simplistic. The Mess Officer is responsible for organizing the potluck dinners or extensive feasts either before, which, although not a normal occurrence, might happen in circumstances determined by the ship, or after ritual. This individual receives monies from the Purser and answers to the Captain for the menu. The Mess Officer is also responsible for choosing the appropriate cakes and wine for the main altar, depending on the ritual. As with most chefs or cooks, the Mess Officer may choose to wear appropriate whites that you would see in a kitchen or a more utilitarian outfit such as long pants and a long-sleeved shirt. Either way, the color would be likely to fit the sterility necessary in a kitchen.

> *The Adjutant is the communications hub for the ship.*

The Adjutant

The Adjutant is the communications hub for the ship. They maintain communication with other covens and airships, issue invitations to rituals, update the website and mailing list, send cards to sick members, and represent the crew in times of discussion with the Captain and Commander. They also convey commands from the Captain to the crew when necessary. If there are changes to a ritual or circle, the Adjutant updates the ship's log (which is the airship's Book of Shadows), and conveys the changes to the crew and other officers.

This individual may dress as they wish, but they are often seen with a notepad and pen, even in ritual.

The Navigator

The final member of the officer staff is the Navigator. The Navigator is responsible for directing the airship, and since the ship is really more of a metaphor, the Navigator has become almost a political officer. When there is news of the area or the ship needs to take a direction in regard to a position within the community, it's the Navigator who researches the options, polls the members, looks at the local and national news concerning this position, and counsels the Captain and the Commander on what is the best option.

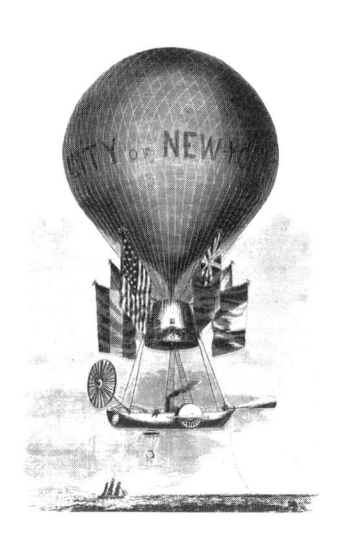

The Navigator may wear anything he chooses since now much of the research conducted is in cyberspace.

※

There are eight officers listed even though there are thirteen members of a full crew. The other five make up the enlisted portion of the crew to carry the metaphor to its conclusion. It is also important to understand that no position is permanent unless the ship chooses to make it such. As in any coven in any other tradition, people move in and out of groups regularly, and promotion or chosen demotion is always available. Therefore do not take these, as I have said about a number of other areas in this book, as locked in or carved in stone forever.

Note: All six officers below the Captain and Commander are of equal rank and are only distinguished by their duties aboard the ship.

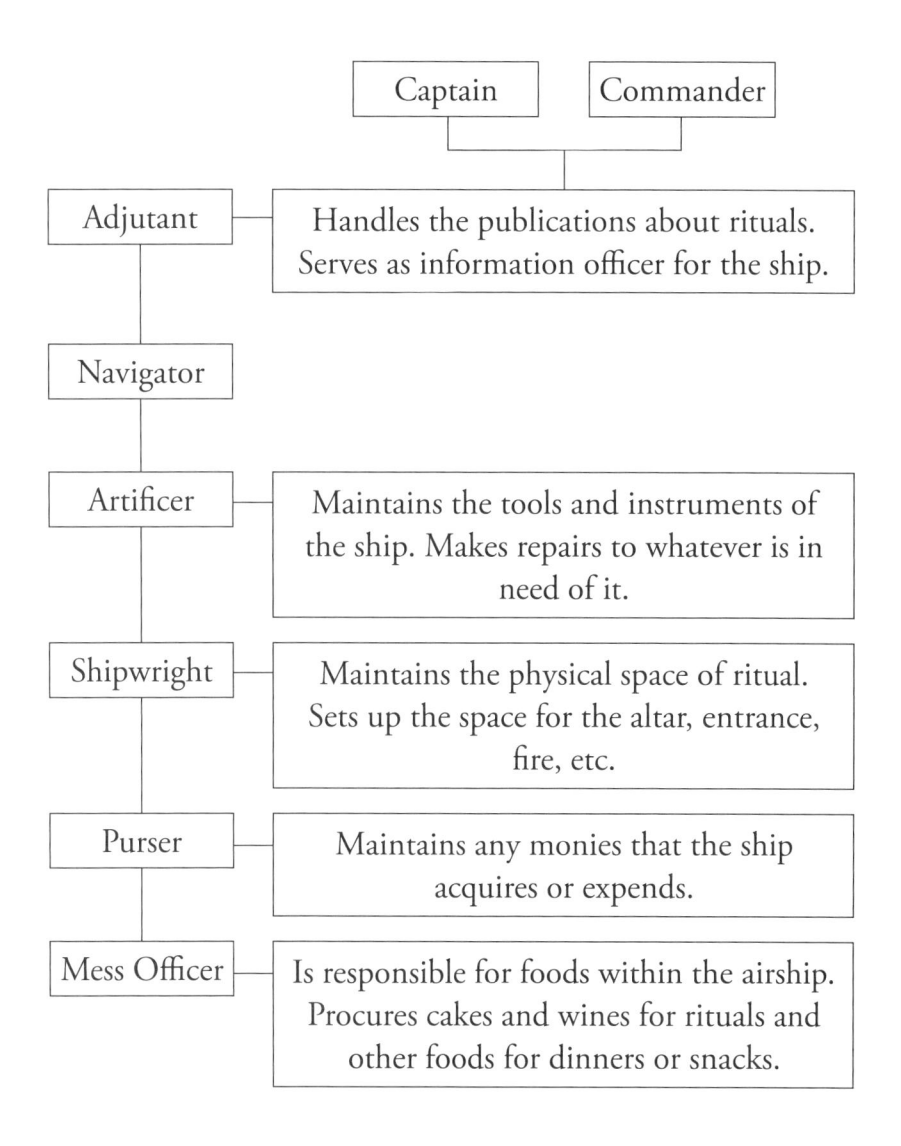

```
        ┌─────────┐  ┌───────────┐
        │ Captain │  │ Commander │
        └─────────┘  └───────────┘
┌──────────┐  ┌──────────────────────────────────────┐
│ Adjutant │──│ Handles the publications about rituals. │
└──────────┘  │ Serves as information officer for the ship. │
              └──────────────────────────────────────┘
┌───────────┐
│ Navigator │
└───────────┘

┌───────────┐  ┌──────────────────────────────────────┐
│ Artificer │──│ Maintains the tools and instruments of │
└───────────┘  │ the ship. Makes repairs to whatever is in │
               │             need of it.              │
               └──────────────────────────────────────┘

┌────────────┐  ┌──────────────────────────────────────┐
│ Shipwright │──│ Maintains the physical space of ritual. │
└────────────┘  │ Sets up the space for the altar, entrance, │
                │             fire, etc.               │
                └──────────────────────────────────────┘

┌────────┐  ┌──────────────────────────────────────┐
│ Purser │──│ Maintains any monies that the ship   │
└────────┘  │         acquires or expends.         │
            └──────────────────────────────────────┘

┌──────────────┐  ┌──────────────────────────────────────┐
│ Mess Officer │──│ Is responsible for foods within the airship. │
└──────────────┘  │ Procures cakes and wines for rituals and │
                  │ other foods for dinners or snacks.   │
                  └──────────────────────────────────────┘
```

Figure 2. The airship crew and their responsibilities.

The Airship and Crew

4
THE TOOLS

Today's scientists have substituted mathematics for experiments, and they wander off through equation after equation, and eventually build a structure which has no relation to reality.

—Nikola Tesla

Many of the tools we use in Steampunk Magic are unique to our system and specifically designed for the applications. I worked construction for a number of years with my uncle in Florida when I was in my late twenties. The crew would often joke, "You can't do the job right if you don't have the tools designed for that operation." And they were correct. A hammer cannot screw in a screw, no matter how many times you hit it. So is it with magic. You might use tools that you think work because you were never taught the difference between a screwdriver and a hammer. This chapter is dedicated to equipping you with everything you need to know to assemble a Steampunk Magic toolkit.

Since we travel in this system through the aether, and that aether is only traversable with proper grounding and equipment, it is essential to understand the tools of the trade, so to speak, and to prepare them for circle. Manufacturers and suppliers of these pieces are either very limited or nonexistent. As a Yankee growing up in New Hampshire I was taught that if I didn't have something I needed and couldn't get it readily, or afford it financially, I made it. I have included some do-it-yourself suggestions for some of these tools for a better understanding of how they are made and how easy it is to create the basic instruments. See figure 3 for an example of all of the tools laid out before ritual.

> *Many of the tools we use in Steampunk Magic are unique to our system and specifically designed for the applications.*

For our purposes, the tools may be as simple as a forefinger or as complex and ornate as gold or silver wands, pentacles, or crystal chalices and dinnerware for cakes and wines.

Let us begin by looking at the materials we'll need to set up the altar.

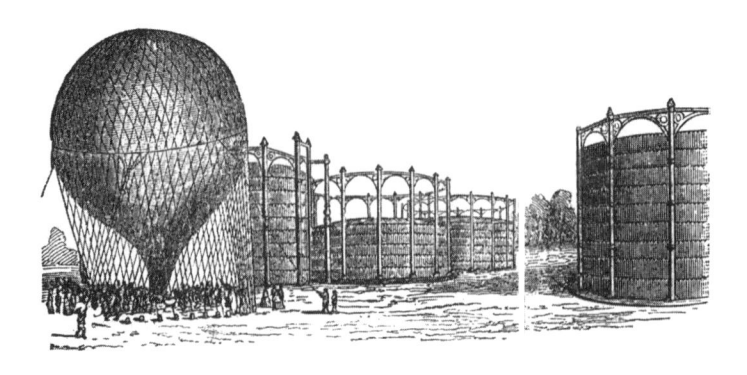

Figure 3. The main altar with all components.

All Steampunk Magic work starts and concludes at north and moves from the inside out in the beginning and from outside in at the conclusion. From the north the circle is cast, and items are placed on the altar in a clockwise manner from the centermost tool to the final one. Let's look at the tools in order of when they are placed on the altar.

Directional Gear

The directional gear is a unique piece of Steampunk Magic. It guides the Captain and Commander through the aether between the realms and keeps them grounded to this plane during all magic work. The directional gear is brass, bronze, or any other nonferrous metal. There are teeth on the gear, and the four cardinal directions are either cast or marked. The size of the gear is at the choice of the airship; however, it should be large enough to hold the compass during setup and the key during ritual. Our compass is in a four-inch square wooden box and our key is six inches in length. So our gear is almost twelve inches in diameter. I have at home, though, a small hunting compass that was my grandfather's that is less than two inches in diameter and not more than three-quarters of an inch in height. The gear necessary to hold that would be significantly smaller.

Building Your Directional Gear

The directional gear is the most difficult item on your alter to build or find. If you cannot find an actual metal gear, you can make one out of wood or thick poster board. There are some very good free images on the Internet for gear patterns that are easy to print out and stencil on the material for cutting. The gear that we use on our airship was specially made using a sand-cast method by Nathan Smith at Clemson University's Art Department Foundry in Clemson, South Carolina. His contact information is at the back of this book. If you aren't lucky enough to find an old gear at an antique auction, or you don't know someone who can make one, you can build a gear from wood or cardboard. Remember that if you use a metal gear, e.g., steel or iron, the compass will give you a false reading and you'll be sailing off course during your circle. Below are a few photos of a gear being poured and completed.

Figure 4. The master copy of the gear.

Figure 5. Pouring the gear in silicate bronze.

Figure 6. The directional gear in rough stage. Needs significant grinding but the overall shape looks good.

Figure 7. The final grinding of the directional gear.

Wand

In most traditions the wand is a section of branch from a tree or shrub. It may be the wood that is sacred to you or your path or one that speaks to you during your early time of initiation. Wands are used to raise and lower energy, open and close the circle in lieu of an athame, and for other kinds of energy direction.

In Steampunk Magic, the wand is different. True it is used to raise and lower energy, direct energy during spell work, and perform other general duties. However, the steampunk wand is made of metal; specifically, a copper or brass tube. At one end is a small, thin quartz crystal for positive energy release; at the other end is a small hematite stone or a matching metal pipe endcap for grounding. Oftentimes the handle of the wand is wrapped in thin leather. For our wands we use copper and wrap them with gold elk hide. Many other wands out in the field are made without wrapping and use the conductivity of the metals directly with the skin. This is another example of you the user making the choice that works best for you.

Steampunk wands come in three sizes, depending on the nature and complexity of the requirements.

Steampunk wands come in three sizes, depending on the nature and complexity of the requirements. An airship should eventually have all three sizes. The largest wand is for public ceremonies where carrying large amounts of energy over wide areas is required. The medium-weight wand is for general use in circle and within the airship. The smallest, most finely-crafted wand is used for healing spell work since that is where very accurate directionality is necessary. The size of the wands may vary with the individual user. Our wands are between twelve and eighteen inches in length.

Building Your Wand

Every wand is built to the requirements of the user, and there are three components to consider: the aft stone, the body of the wand, and the fore crystal. See figure 8 to compare the three sizes of wands. The largest wand is not that much larger than the wand used in circle, so don't get caught up with size.

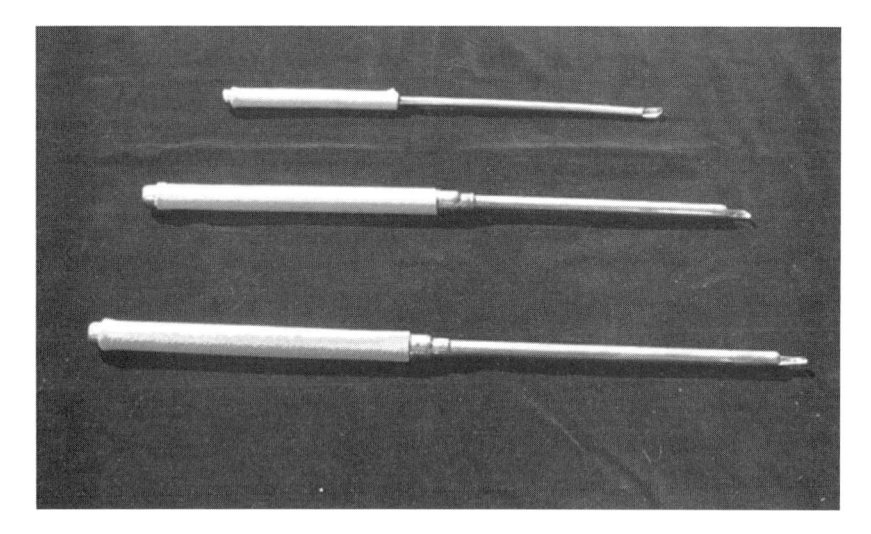

Figure 8. Three wands side by side. We chose to cap the aft end of the wands with metal and wrap the handles in gold elk hide.

Goggles

Sight is essential when sailing through the aether, Goggles enhance the sight of the practitioner and enable the individual to perceive obstacles that may be looming beyond normal vision. Goggles may be as simple as a pair of safety goggles purchased from a hardware store or as complex as a handmade set of brass, with ground lenses and leather attachments custom ordered or built by the initiate. Regardless of the origin of the goggles, they are the vision of the ceremony and very important to much of the Steampunk Magic spell work since they allow the Captain, Commander, or airship member the ability to see more than what is readily shown.

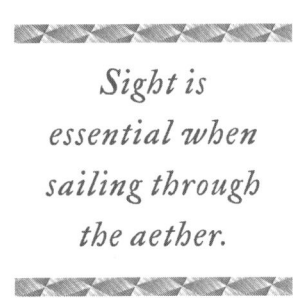

> *Sight is essential when sailing through the aether.*

Building Your Goggles

Included here are three ideas for goggles. The first is a very simple design for those who don't have much space or the tools to make a more elaborate pair. The second design is for those who have a little more time; it uses fabric. And the third design is advanced, for those who are very creative and have leather and metal tools at their disposal.

PAPER TOWEL ROLL GOGGLES

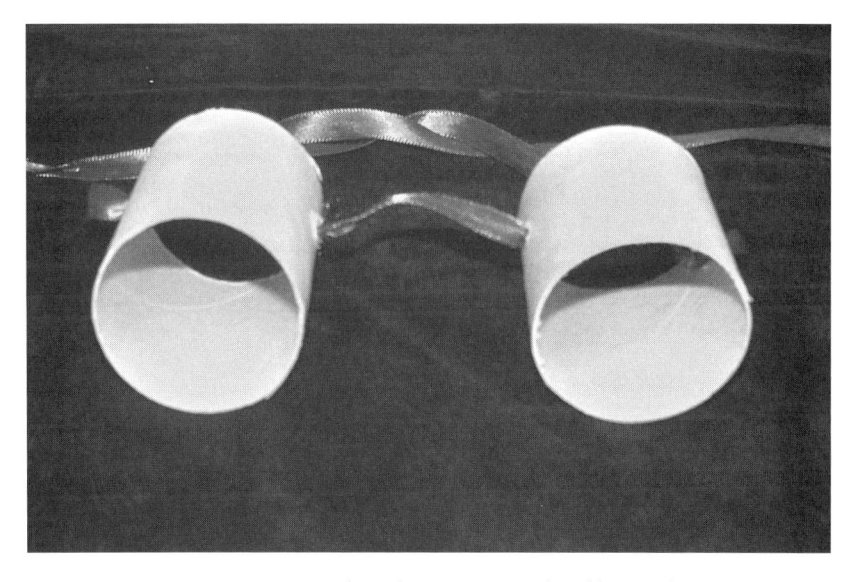

Figure 9. Completed paper towel roll goggles.

For this design you will need:

- A paper towel roll or toilet paper roll
- Single-hole punch
- Some string
- A pair of scissors or razor knife
- A hot glue gun or other glue

Cut two sections of the paper roll, each approximately one and one-half inches long. Punch a small hole in the center of each piece on both sides of the roll large enough for the string to fit through. Cut one piece of string approximately three inches long for the nosepiece and two pieces approximately fourteen inches long for the head straps. Place the two paper pieces side by side, and run the small piece of string through one hole in each piece. There should be enough space between the two rolls that you can wear the rolls similar to a pair of glasses. Knot the string. Glue the knot so it doesn't come undone. Take each of the longer pieces of string and run one piece through each side hole of the rolls, then knot and glue. When you need the goggles for visioning you may tie them on and proceed.

CLOTH-COVERED PAPER ROLL GOGGLES

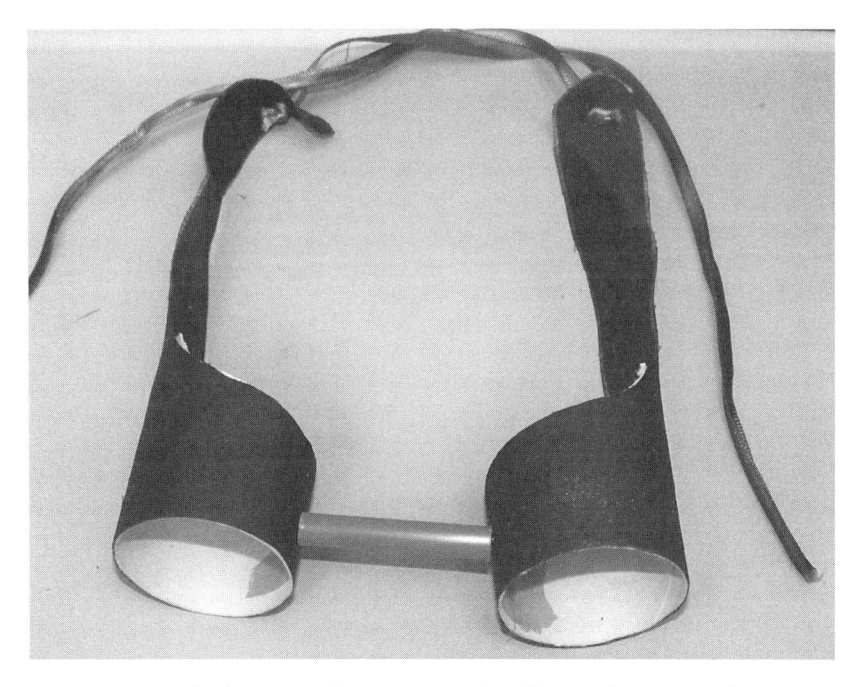

Figure 10. Cloth-covered paper towel roll goggles. Note the straw for the nosepiece and fitted cloth covering.

If you have light canvas or trigger cloth around the house, or if you have access to very light leather, you can make a more lasting pair of goggles still using the paper towel rolls.

For this design you will need:

- A paper towel roll or toilet paper roll
- Fabric or leather
- Single-hole punch

- Some string
- A pair of scissors or razor knife
- One drinking straw
- A hot glue gun or other glue

Cut two sections of the paper roll, each approximately one and one-half inches long. Cut two covers for the paper roll pieces that are the same dimensions as the rolls, and glue the fabric or leather to the rolls. Punch a small hole in the center of each roll on both sides of the roll large enough for the string to fit through. Cut one piece of string approximately three inches long for the nosepiece and two pieces approximately fourteen inches long for the head straps. You may roll a piece of cloth around a drinking straw and run the short piece of string through the straw to make the nosepiece more attractive. Place the two paper pieces side by side, and run the small piece of string through one hole in each piece. There should be enough space between the two rolls that you can wear the rolls similar to a pair of glasses. Knot the string. Glue the knot so it doesn't come undone. Take each of the longer pieces of string and run one piece through each side hole of the rolls, then knot and glue. Then either cut the coverings long enough to attach a buckle or tie the pieces off with latigo or rat tail that you can purchase at a fabric or hobby store.

METAL AND LEATHER GOGGLES

These are more involved, but they will last for years and look good doing it.

For this design you will need:

- A 2-inch double connector for sinks
- Heavy leather or heavy-duty canvas
- A 1-inch buckle
- Rivets
- Rivet setter
- Metal punch or drill
- Heavy sewing lace, such as artificial sinew
- A sewing needle
- Heavy-duty hole punch that can go through leather or heavy canvas
- A ¾-inch Chicago screw
- A ¾-inch piece of copper tubing
- Two 2-inch glass lenses

Cut the plumbing piece at the end of the widest area (see figures 11–14). This gives you two eyepieces. Cut the leather or heavy canvas to cover the eyepieces and long enough to extend to the back of your head for the buckle. Remember to leave enough length on one of the pieces for the buckle to fold back on itself, and at the other piece for holes to adjust the goggles to your head. Glue or rivet the coverings to the eyepieces and set aside to dry. After drying, punch a hole in each piece of goggle directly across from the center of your outside strap for the nosepiece. The holes must be large enough for the shaft of the Chicago screw but not as large as the copper tubing. Run the screw through the eyepiece from the inside out, through the tube, then back into the other eyepiece, and screw tightly. You may finally find two 2-inch glass lenses at the hobby shop for flashlights that will fit in the screw sections of the goggles.

Figure 11. The plumbing piece intact.

Figure 12. The plumbing piece in the vise.

Figure 13. One eyepiece cut.

Figure 14. Both eyepieces cut.

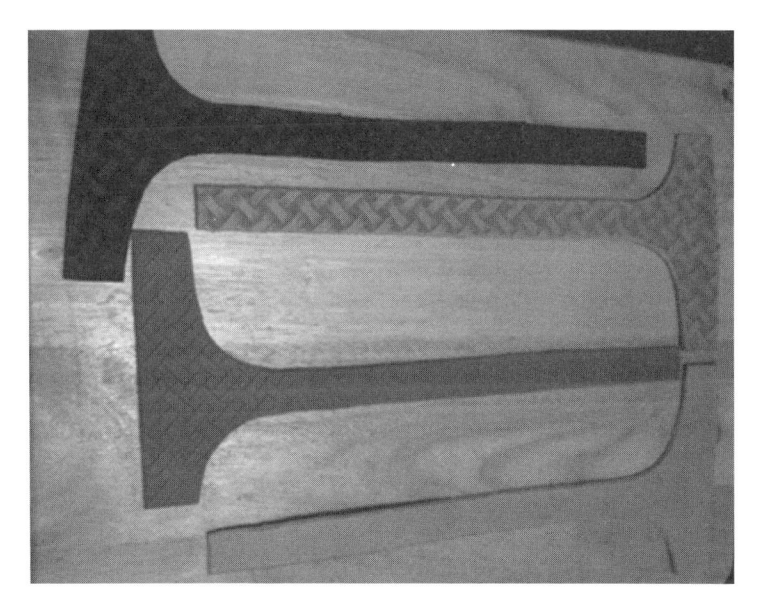

Figure 15. Four stages of the goggle straps; plain, pattern cut, pattern tooled, strap stained.

Figure 16. Goggle eyepieces trimmed with gold elk hide.

The Tools

Figure 17. Completed goggles with nosepiece and buckle attached. These pieces only used one rivet.

Cakes and Wine

Cakes and wine are an important part of most circles, and in Steampunk Magic we are no different. They are the nourishment of the body as the circle is nourishment of the spirit. The cakes may be scones, small cakes, or cookies. Victorian Lace Cookies are easy to make and very authentic. For wine, I recommend absinthe. For non-drinkers, tea can substitute for wine.

VICTORIAN LACE COOKIES

Lace cookies are a good choice for "cakes" at Steampunk Magic circles. They are very fragile and dainty but also very attractive on a silver plate. The tiny holes created as they bake look similar to chair lace when sifted with confectioner's sugar.

Ingredients:

- ½ cup corn syrup
- ½ cup unsalted butter
- ⅔ cup brown sugar
- 1 cup flour
- Confectioner's sugar for topping

Mix corn syrup, unsalted butter, and brown sugar in a saucepan and heat until the mixture comes to a boil. Mix in flour, approximately 1 cup, or until you get a good cookie consistency. Preheat oven to 325 degrees. Drop teaspoon size portions of cookie dough on a greased baking sheet and cook for 10 minutes. Allow cookies to cool before removing from baking sheet, since they will be less likely to break apart after one or two minutes.

VICTORIAN SCONES

The scone is a staple at most Victorian or English tea parties and may make a good "cake" for the Steampunk circle. Scones are basically a biscuit, although lighter than a traditional American one, and are prepared similarly.

Ingredients:

- 2 cups flour
- 1 Tbsp baking powder
- 2 Tbsp sugar
- ½ tsp salt
- 3 Tbsp butter
- 1 egg, beaten
- ¾ cup milk
- Melted butter

Preheat oven to 450 degrees. Combine the flour, baking powder, sugar, salt, butter, and egg in a large bowl. Slowly add the milk while stirring until the mixture takes on a dough consistency. Put dough on a floured cutting board and knead until it is ready to cut. Roll out the dough to approximately one-half to three quarters of an inch and use a 2-inch biscuit or doughnut cutter to create the scones. Place each scone on a nonstick baking sheet. Baste lightly with melted butter and bake at 450 degrees for 12 minutes. Check regularly to avoid burning. Remove from oven when cooked and lightly butter the tops before serving.

Contrary to many past thoughts, absinthe is no more dangerous than any other liquor. Story has it that when the French troops returned home after World War I, the burgeoning French wine industry was floundering under the popularity of the Green Fairy. With some very large and carefully targeted financial gifts that some called bribes, the rumor that absinthe was deadly spread until eventually the drink became illegal. This made the French wines and champagnes regain their popularity. However, there is nothing in absinthe that is toxic to the consumer, and different brands are now available at most liquor stores.

Absinthe has a strong black licorice taste due to the anise used in its distillation process. It also has a high alcohol-to-liquid ratio, and for that reason it is often diluted with water or another mixer. Combine the licorice flavor and the high alcohol content, and the ritual of preparing absinthe was created. For ritual you may either prepare absinthe in the traditional way, dripping ice-cold water over a sugar cube that is held above the glass of absinthe with a specially-shaped spoon (an absinthe spoon), or you may "cheat" and prepare simple syrup prior to the ritual and mix the absinthe with the water and simple syrup. Either way you should keep the glass of absinthe chilled on the altar in a bowl of ice during warmer months.

> *Absinthe has a strong black licorice taste due to the anise used in its distillation process.*

ABSINTHE RITUAL

If you aren't able to perform the full ritual of absinthe, you may use super-cooled simple syrup. However, there is something very traditional about watching the full ritual play out at a ceremony, so I have included our take on the ritual as well as a shorter but still traditional version.

Ingredients:

- 1.5 ounces absinthe
- Reservoir glass, wineglass, or any other barware glass
- 1 sugar cube
- Absinthe spoon or tea strainer
- 4.5–7.5 ounces ice-cold water

Pour the absinthe into the glass. Place a sugar cube on top of the absinthe spoon, then either place or hold the spoon over the glass. Slowly pour or drip ice-old water over the sugar cube until the sugar has dissolved into the absinthe below. The final preparation traditionally contains about 1 part absinthe and 3–5 parts water.

An absinthe spoon is a finely-slotted spoon that is flat and often has a bottom lip to keep the spoon from slipping into the glass. If you cannot find an absinthe spoon, any open or slotted spoon may work. You may also try using a tea strainer—the type that fits over a tea cup with a wire hook on one end to keep the strainer stable on the cup.

For dedicated absinthe drinkers, an absinthe fountain filled with iced water can be used. The spigot of the fountain is placed directly over the sugar cube and a fine drizzle or steady stream of cold water is set up to strike the sugar cube. When the cube is dissolved in the glass the absinthe is ready to drink.

Alternatively, you can make your own absinthe fountain. To do this, wrap a few ice cubes in a piece of cheesecloth and place that in the tea strainer. As the ice melts it will dissolve the sugar cube and perform the absinthe ritual effectively, if not aesthetically.

Absinthe is best served very cold. You may choose to omit the sugar if you wish or use the sugar and omit the water. Absinthe, as with any other drinks, is at the pleasure of the consumer.

For those who choose to not consume alcoholic beverages, Earl Grey tea works very well. It is a fine English tea that complements scones and cookies and retains the tradition of cakes and wine without straying far from the more frequently used grape or apple juice alternative.

Rigging Knife

The rigging knife is the working knife of the system. In traditional times the boline was a circular single blade knife used to cut herbs and other plants for ritual and potions (see figure 18).

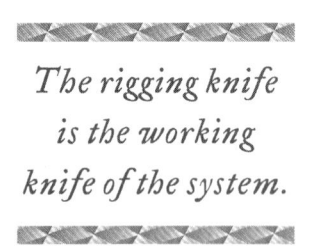

The rigging knife is the working knife of the system.

The handle was traditionally white for the purity that was necessary during preparation. There are very few circular knives currently in production, and on an airship a scythe would be less practical as a working knife.

Most likely your rigging knife will be a single straight blade with a sawtooth or serrated pattern on the spine. This gives the knife a sharp front edge for cutting and a more industrial back edge for heavy sawing. The handle may be any color and any material as long as it is comfortable and nonslip. A good knife for general use may be any you would carry on a naval or airship, since cutting rigging and sails is much more wearing on a knife than cutting herbs and candles and you want your knife to last for as long as you practice magic.

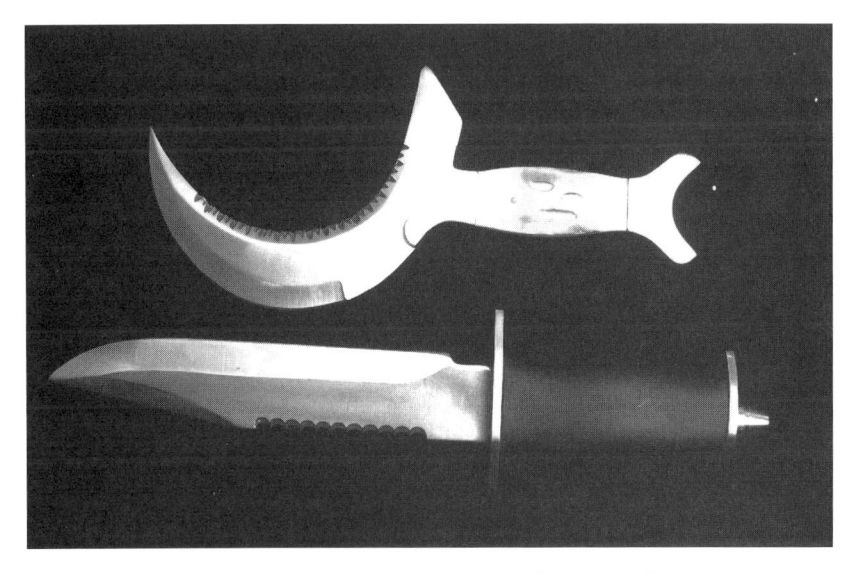

Figure 18. The traditional boline (top) and rigging knife (bottom).

Compass

The compass has been a navigational aide for over 2,000 years. You may use the traditional 360-degree compass or the 6400 radian compass that the artillery and other combat arms in the military use—either one is fine. Every compass displays the four cardinal directions: north, south, east, and west. These correspond to the four directions and gateways of the traditional magic circle. The compass is used in the circle to draw direction to the objective and destination. It is the principal device for aligning divination and is used prior to ritual to orient the directional gear on the altar, thus aligning all other aspects of the circle. The compass always points to magnetic north, therefore it is a tool of the north.

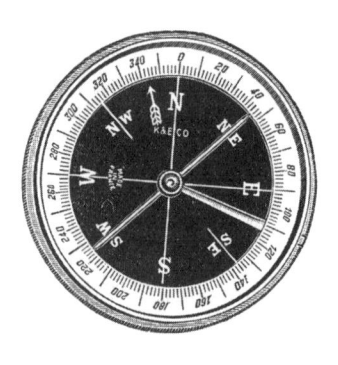

Spike

The spike is the steampunk version of the athame. (The spike or the wand may be used interchangeably. In magic, wands and athames are often at the choice of the practitioner.) In ancient times the athame was the ceremonial knife for opening and closing circle. Alternatively used with a wand, these single blade knives with dark handles represented the masculine god of the circle and penetrated the goddess during ritual.

The spike may be a double-edged blade of brass, bronze, or copper. The handle is usually dark wood. There may also be no handle at all, just the forged blade of metal.

Another tool that is applicable would be a spike-ended open wrench or closed wrench in brass or bronze. These wrenches were used on airships or in engine rooms, where sparks could be fatal. Like the blade of an athame, the spike or wrench is directly tied to the earth and the energies within. Even though the spike is forged from the ores of the earth it shines with the sun and therefore may be thought of as a northern or eastern tool.

Lamp

The lamp lights the way through the darkness of the aether. It is a brass and/or glass oil-burning device that is lit during opening ceremony. It is an instrument of light, and so despite its earthen metals or glass it remains an instrument of the east.

Gas/Air

Gas and hot air lift. We are buoyed into the aether by this eastern element. Helium is the gas of choice, but hot air is just as practical, though it doesn't last as long. Air may be represented by a small airship model, a steam generator, or a small balloon tethered to a stone representing our connection to the earth.

Censer

The censer is the heat of the ship. It is the fire that transforms water into steam to drive our society and heats air to lift our ships. The censer may be a small brass dish for incense or another flame/heat-producing element.

Water

Water powers all actions through steam. It also purifies all tools and members of the circle. Water makes up the vast majority of all living things; from water we are born, and to water we shall pass. Water is held in a brass or glass bowl.

Salt Cellar

Salt is an interesting compound. Although it is found in the ocean in abundance, it is mined in the earth more than from the seas. It may be represented in a dish or in a large cube.

MAKE YOUR OWN SALT CRYSTALS

As a child my grandmother and I would make rock candy. You could buy these large crystals of pure sugar from the store and skip the day of cooking and cooling it takes to make rock candy at home, but it was more fun doing it the old-fashioned way. My grandmother and I would dissolve sugar in water and keep stirring until the sugar water was almost syrup. Then we'd turn the heat off and I'd watch the crystals forming as the water cooled. You now pretty much have the recipe for making salt crystals.

I like to use rock salt for making larger crystals. For some reason the crystals form more solid than using household salt, although that works, too. All salt, like sugar, is a crystalline substance and will grow appropriately.

You will need:

- 2 quarts water
- Approximately 1-½ cups rock salt
- Sanitized glass wide-mouthed jar, such as an orange or tomato juice jar, with lid
- Small salt crystal
- Sewing thread
- Toothpick

Place a 2-quart pot of water on the stove and bring to a boil. Add 1 cup of salt, and stir until the salt is dissolved. Slowly add more salt—1 or 2 tablespoons at a time—until you don't think the water can hold any more dissolved crystals. Pour the hot water into the glass jar. Make certain the jar is sanitized completely. Finally, tie the small salt crystal to the bottom of a piece of sewing thread and suspend the string in the liquid. I like to punch a small hole in the top of the lid and tie the other end to a toothpick.

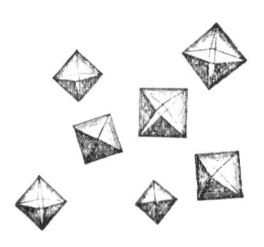

Place the jar in a cool (but not cold) section of your house and the crystals will start to form. When the crystals reach between nickel and quarter size you may remove the thread and after drying the crystals you may use them as you need. This process may take twenty minutes or longer, depending on the altitude and the amount of salt dissolved.

If you have small children around the house you might want to do this with sugar also. It's cheaper than candy and fun to make.

Key

Every engine starts with a key. Every idea begins with a key. Every lock is opened or closed with a key. The key is the symbol of Steampunk Magic. The steampunk key is more than just a traditional key on a chain—it is actually very similar to a wand, but much smaller.

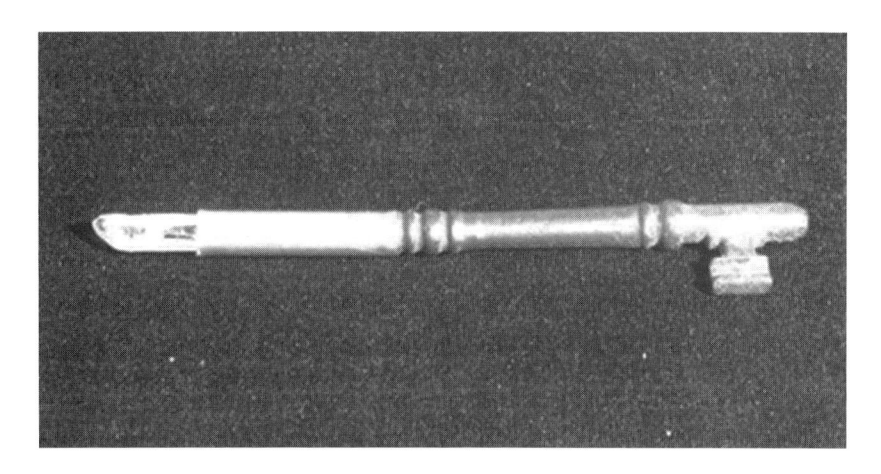

Figure 19. A Steampunk Magic key.

There are three components of the key: the crystal, the shaft, and the key itself. At one end of the key is the airship's stone or crystal of choice. This may be a quartz crystal to focus the energy of the key, or it may be any other stone or crystal that the airship has determined best represents their purpose. For a full list of crystals and stones, I recommend Scott Cunningham's *Encyclopedia of Crystal, Gem and Metal Magic*. The shaft of the key is approximately three inches long and is made of very small copper, brass, or bronze tubing. At the aft end of the key is an actual key portion that is fitted into the tube to form what would look like a standard key.

BUILDING YOUR KEY

Making a key is at about the same level of difficulty as making the wand but easier to build than the goggles.

You will need:

- A skeleton key, preferably one made of nonferrous metal, such as brass or bronze
- One 3-inch section of copper or brass tubing; the inside diameter should be slightly larger than the shaft of the skeleton key
- A stone or crystal of your choice
- Soldering iron and solder or a silicon-based epoxy

Using either a hacksaw, a metal cutting blade in an X-Acto handle, or a rotary tool, cut the key at the handle section, giving you the longest shaft possible. Solder or epoxy the key shaft inside one end of the copper tube. If you use an epoxy try to make certain it is a silicone base. The silicone is more elemental and therefore will conduct energy batter than some of the other available epoxies on the market. At the other end attach the stone or crystal. For our ship we use a small quartz crystal that fits inside the brass tube.

Storing Your Tools

Your tools can easily get scattered if left by themselves throughout crew members' houses and yards. Therefore I keep all of the altar pieces in a series of boxes specifically designed for them. See figures 20 and 21 for two of the boxes I made for my ship. The larger box is for the smaller pieces, such as the directional gear, compass, and other tools. I have another slightly larger box for the steam/gas producer and the dish for the cakes. I also made a gearbox for the tarot deck.

Figure 20. A tooled leather storage box for the major altar pieces.

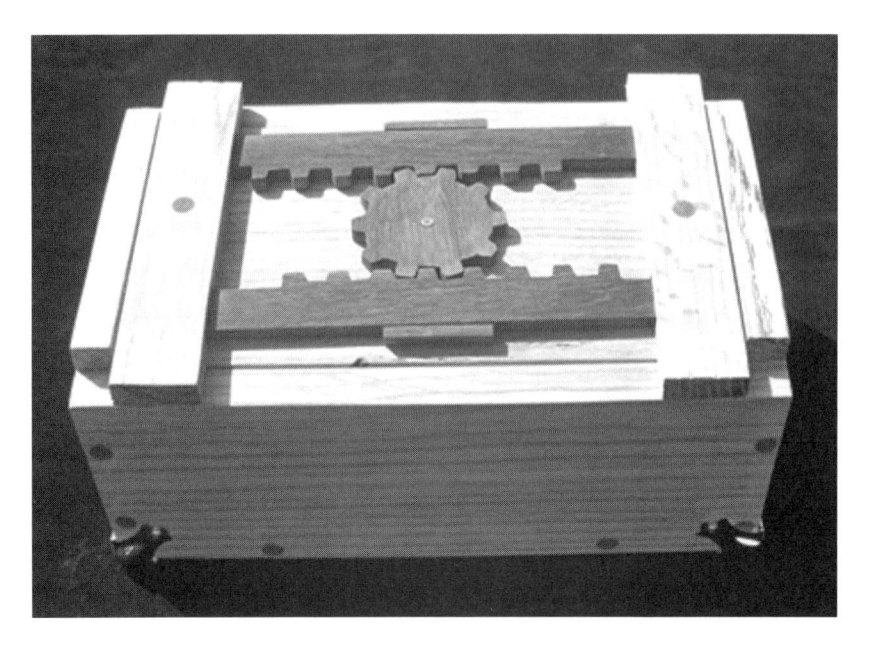

Figure 21. A tarot deck storage box made of red oak and purpleheart. The gear on top opens and closes the sidebars that lock the box.

5

PREPARING THE ALTARS AND CASTING THE CIRCLE

Science is always discovering odd scraps of magical wisdom and making a tremendous fuss about its cleverness.
—Aleister Crowley

Before a circle may be cast, the space must be prepared, and the altars must be set up. The day of ritual the Shipwright will arrive first. It is his/her job to prepare the physical space that the ritual will take place in. If the circle is outside, then weeding may be needed, or repairs to walls, patio blocks, or painting may be in order. If the ritual is inside, sweeping and dusting is required. As the maintenance individual for the ship's rituals, this preparatory phase is one of the most important times that the Shipwright will be needed. Preparing the space beforehand is essential: without it the ritual will lack feeling.

Next the Artificer will arrive with the magic box. In my airship we keep all of our altar tools in a large wooden box that I made. The Artificer will align the altar and then arrange each piece as needed. Once the Shipwright and the Artificer agree that the space and altars are ready, they will report to the Captain that the circle is ready to be cast.

Assembling the Main Altar

The main altar is round and approximately thirty-six inches in diameter. We begin with two concentric rings drawn around a central circle. The center circle is just large enough to place the directional gear within. The next two rings may be separated six inches at a minimum or as great as twelve inches.

In Steampunk Magic we use slightly different tools to represent the elements.

I have found that the larger the distance between lines, the better. If you have room, a thirty-six-inch table is ideal; some altar items, such as the directional gear, the rigging knife, and the cakes and wine take up a goodly amount of space.

Lines do not need to be drawn on the altar cloth or on the altar itself, though it may help when setting up the altar for instructional purposes with the initiates. These rings are your elemental markings. If your directional gear does not have the four cardinal directions marked, you may want to mark north, south, east, and west on the altar cloth. These four elemental directions correspond with earth, air, fire, and water (see chart on page 88).

In Steampunk Magic we use slightly different tools to represent the elements. Air is a good example. In many traditions air is represented with a candle or a feather at times. In Steampunk Magic air is also referred to as gas and is represented by either a hot air producer such as a candle, or a small helium balloon that shows the lifting capabilities of the gas. Another example is the use of coal as a representative of fire. Most traditions use a burner, which we do also in some instances; however, it's the coal that burns to allow our ships to rise with hot air so coal, from the earth, still represents fire.

The outer ring is for those tools that are specifically of one element. A piece of hematite is purely earth. It has magnetic properties and comes from the earth. Hematite would be placed squarely at the earth element on the outer ring. Another example of a pure element would be fire. A burning brazier, albeit a small one, burning is the fire element in its natural state. Other such tools and elements are placed on the outer ring as to their properties.

The inner circle is for finer tuning of your elemental placement. If an item has both fire and earth elements associated with it, and earth is the more dominant, then the item would be placed on the inner circle at the north, but where it would also be associated with fire. As an example, let's look at the wand. The wand is made of brass and copper, both earth elements. However, the tubing that makes up the shaft of the wand is formed by smelting the ores into the final configuration. Therefore, fire is used. With earth as the primary element and fire as the secondary element, the wand would be placed on the inner circle at north.

Another example of placement would be if a tool is equal in elementals. The spike is made from brass but shines with the power of the sun. Therefore, it is placed equidistant from the earth and the air/sun elements or north and east. Each tool and instrument is placed in such a manner.

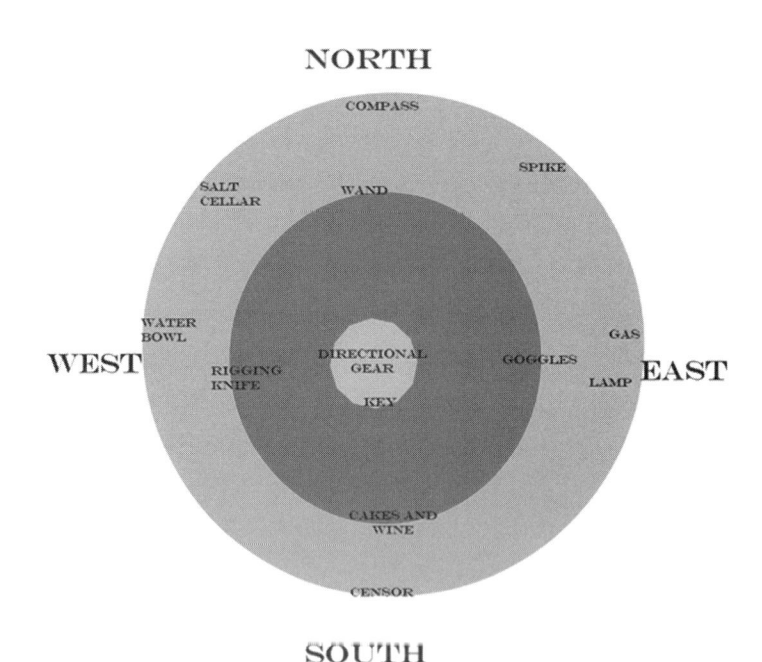

Figure 22. Tool placement on the altar.

Remember, all Steampunk Magic work begins and concludes at north. In the beginning things move from the inside out, at the conclusion from the outside in. The circle is cast from the north, and items are placed on the altar in a clockwise manner, from the centermost tool to the final one.

> The **directional gear** is the first item placed on the altar and the last item removed. Since it is the most essential piece on the altar it is aligned with the compass. It is an actual gear placed at the center of the altar, and aligned with a compass to point to the four cardinal directions and subsequently align the inner and outer ring of the altar for placement of other tools.
>
> The **wand** is crafted from ores and metals of the earth in furnaces of heat and fire. It is placed on the inner ring of the north element and may be pointed in any direction at the choice of the Captain using it.

Preparing the Altars and Casting the Circle

Goggles are instruments of sight and therefore can be used to see the light of travel; but they are also used to peer into the void. They are placed on the inner ring of the eastern element where the sunrise will open the eyes of the viewer as they pierce the aether.

Since the **cakes and wine** are created with produce from the earth and prepared with fire from the ovens and boilers, they go on the altar at the inner ring of the fire element.

The **rigging knife** is forged of the earth metals and ores. However, it is tempered for its hardness with fire and water to form a tool rugged enough to withstand years of use. The rigging knife is placed on the inner ring of the altar on the west side equal distance between north and south and may be pointed in any direction on the altar as per the choice of the Captain performing the circle.

The **compass** always points to magnetic north, therefore it is a tool of the North. Place the compass in the outer ring of the altar at the north point, in alignment with the directional gear.

The **spike** is placed on the outer ring at the northeast point of the altar. Similar to the wand and the rigging knife, the spike may be pointed in whatever direction is best applicable to the user.

The **lamp** is placed in the eastern outer ring.

Gas is placed on the outer ring at the eastern element. On our altar we use a distiller, which is an old glass water heater over a heat source to create steam that lifts our ships. It is large but we have adapted to it over the years since we found it in an antique store. I have found it's safer at times to have a distiller, because a balloon may blow too close to the lamp and pop at the most inopportune moment during circle.

The **censer** is a fire element and is placed on the outer ring at the southern point.

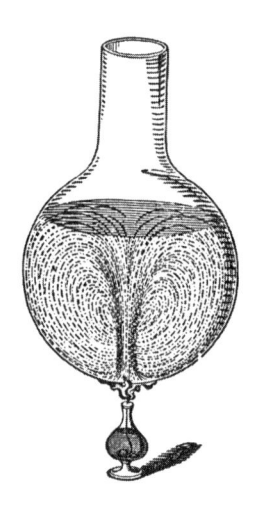

Preparing the Altars and Casting the Circle

Water is held in a brass or glass bowl. It is a western element and is placed at the western point of the outer ring.

For **salt**, you must include both the west and the north for healing and ritualistic properties. The salt cellar is placed on the altar at the northwest point of the outer ring.

The **key** is the point of beginning and the final point of ending the ceremony. It is placed in the center of the directional gear. Everything that comes before the key is placed on the directional gear prior to casting the circle, and everything that happens after the key is removed from the directional gear at the end of the circle is administrative. We also cast with the key since it is the focal point of the altar. This is not carved in stone, however, and there are other times when in a large public circle we have used the larger wand. But for most of the ship's rituals the Captain will cast with the key.

If your ritual will involve something that is not normally on the altar, such as a tarot deck, pendulum, or other divination tool, then you may leave a space and determine the proximity of the item to its most logical element(s).

The Quarters

Quarters are arranged after the main altar is assembled and before the key is used to cast the circle. Each quarter altar will have a candle and a representative of the quarter. Steampunk Magic uses a traditional approach to the quarters and their colors and properties:

Direction	Properties	Color
North	Earth	Brown, for the earth
East	Air	Yellow, for the sun
South	Fire	Red, for the fire
West	Water	Blue, for the waters

For this action, you will need:

- Brown candle
- Piece of hematite or lodestone
- Yellow candle

Preparing the Altars and Casting the Circle

- Hot air producer or small helium balloon
- Red candle
- Small piece of coal
- Blue candle
- Small water dish or water bottle

Using the directional gear, identify the four cardinal directions and place your quarter altars.

North Quarter Altar: Place a brown candle on the north altar. In front of that place a piece of hematite or lodestone (also known as magnetite).

East Quarter Altar: Place a yellow candle on the east altar. In front of that place a hot air producer or small helium balloon. Use caution when using a balloon on the altar. Keep the balloon well tethered to prevent it from coming too close to the flame of the candle.

South Quarter Altar: Place a red candle on the south altar. In front of that place a small piece of coal.

West Quarter Altar: Place a blue candle on the west altar. In front of that place a small water dish or water bottle.

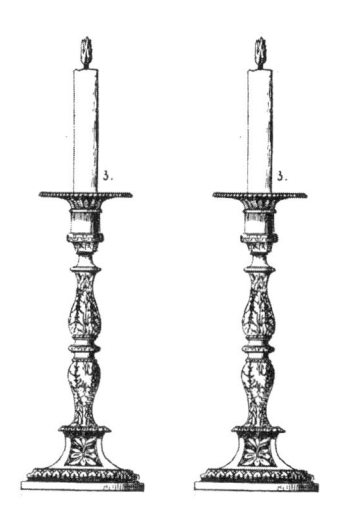

The Steam Up and Steam Down Salutes

The salute that is given at the beginning and ending of many rituals and circles, quarters, and other spell work is representative of the power of steam and the closeness of steam to the aether. We pay homage to the power that lifts our ships and our spirits by invoking the Salute of Steam.

Steam Up: Facing the element, clap hands together at chest level and then move hands upward and outward, ending with hands being shoulder width with arms fully extended.

Steam Down: Facing the element, begin with arms fully extended and hands shoulder-width apart. Bring down your hands to chest level ending with both hands touching, palms inward.

Casting the Circle

The circle is where most of the work is performed. It is a safe and protected area where your airship may convene, work their magic, and be secure from outside influences. The circle that is cast in Steampunk Magic is very similar to other traditions but in a somewhat different order of occurrence. The Captain casts the circle with the key first. Then the Captain orders the circle cleansed and the quarters called. At each quarter the crew member assigned the task, and these individuals may change as the situation dictates since not everyone is always available at every ritual, welcomes the gods and spirits of that element and direction into the circle to be part of the magical work. Finally, when all are assembled, gods, spirits, and members, the circle is declared closed and work may begin.

In ballooning terms, the envelope is the actual balloon that lifts whatever is beneath it.

With the key the Captain walks clockwise from north and says:

> I cast thee circle to be smooth and endless, devoid of teeth and burr. A circle that protects those within in a sacred and beneficial envelope.

In this case the word "envelope" refers to the entire bubble that is created when a circle is cast. In ballooning terms, the envelope is the actual balloon that lifts whatever is beneath it.

The material is composed of a number of parts, but when taken in its entirety the term used is envelope. Once the Captain has cast the circle, he places the key on the center of the directional gear to signify that the circle is cast.

Note: In most other traditions and systems, the circle is cleansed before being cast. In Steampunk Magic we are operating on a ship. We believe that the ship should be air ready before any other duties are performed, and so we cast the circle before cleansing to ensure that the ship is aether-worthy. In nautical terms, you might say that we have cast off the ropes and set sail prior to setting a course heading and lowering the sails.

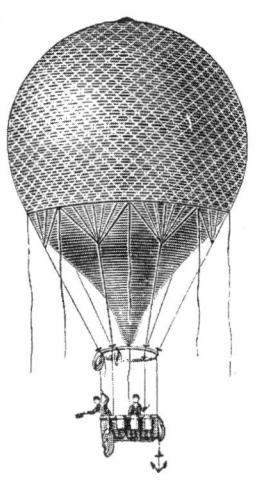

Cleansing the Circle

Once the circle has been cast, the Captain calls the Commander forward. The Captain orders the Commander to prepare the circle for ritual. The first duty of the Commander is to call the Shipwright to cleanse the circle.

The Shipwright takes the lamp from the altar and starting in the north in a clockwise direction says:

> I light the way from this plane through the aether. All obstacles shall be identified.

The Shipwright then returns the lamp and takes the salt cellar from the altar. Starting in the north, the Shipwright sprinkles salt in a clockwise direction and says:

I strike all the obstacles in our path. Only clear skies shall remain.

He or she then returns the salt cellar and takes the water bowl from the altar. Starting in the north, he or she spritzes water in a clockwise direction and says:

I cleanse this circle of all negativity. Only peace and love shall enter.

The Shipwright returns the water bowl. At this point the Shipwright reports to the Commander that the circle has been cleansed. The Commander thanks the Shipwright, and the Shipwright returns to the general assemblage.

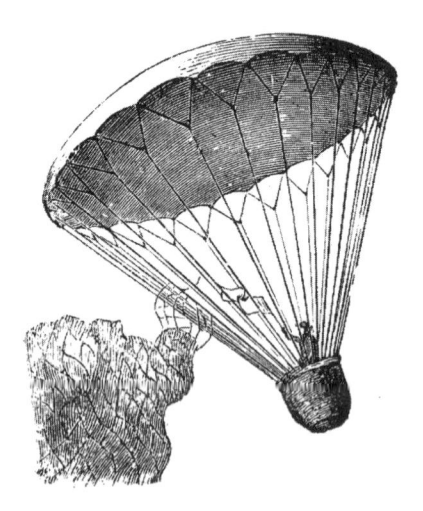

Calling the Quarters

Next the Commander calls forth the Artificer so that that the quarters can be called. The Artificer calls as many members of the crew as deemed necessary, usually four others, to call quarters. Each crew member takes their place at a quarter and under the guiding eye of the Artificer they begin at the north.

North Quarter Altar

Facing the elemental altar, the member says:

> Gods and spirits of the north. We invite you to come out of your factories, your foundries, and your deep earthen mines. Bring your copper, your tin, and your zinc; your wrenches and your tools. Join our rite and protect those who are within the circle.

> The member then lights the candle.

East Quarter Altar

Facing the elemental altar, the member says:

> Gods and spirits of the east. We invite you to come down from your airships, from your gaseous realm of hot air, helium, and hydrogen. Bring your envelopes and your propellers; your lift machines and your altimeters. Join our rite and protect those that are within the circle.

> The member then lights the candle.

South Quarter Altar

Facing the elemental altar, the member says:

> Gods and sprits of the south. We invite you to come up from your coal mines that light our fires and lift our ships, and your furnaces that melt our metals. Join our rite and protect those that are within the circle.

The member then lights the candle.

West Quarter Altar

Facing the elemental altar, the member says:

> Gods and spirits of the west. We invite you to leave your water that fills our tanks and your steam that drives our ships. Travel through frozen realms and misty clouds to join our rite and protect those that are within the circle.

The member then lights the candle.

At this point the Artificer dismisses the quarters crew and they return to the general assemblage. The Artificer then reports to the Commander that the quarters are cast. The Commander thanks the Artificer and dismisses him/her to the general assemblage. The Commander turns to the Captain and reports:

> Sir, the circle has been cleansed and the quarters have been called. The ship is prepared to sail.

The Captain thanks the Commander and dismisses the Commander, who returns to the general assemblage unless he or she is needed for the circle. The Captain then faces inward from the north quarter and says to the crew:

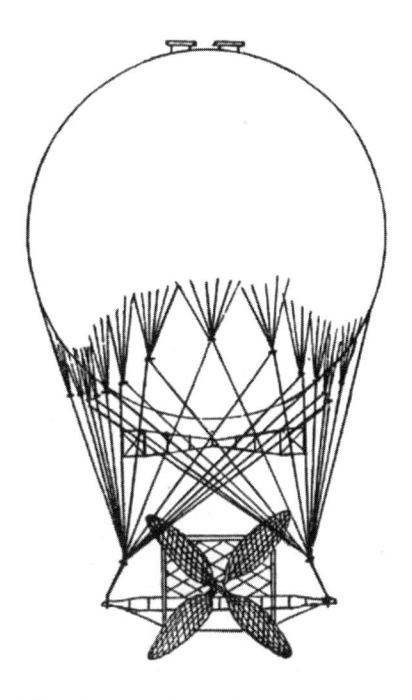

> The circle in cast, the gears are set in motion, and we move forward into the aether. Steam up.

All members of the circle perform the Steam Up salute and say in unison:

> Steam up.

When the magical work is concluded, it is imperative that the circle be disassembled and all gods and spirits thanked properly. The disassembling of the circle is basically a reversal of the assembly.

Opening the Circle

At the end of the circle the Captain calls for the Commander. The Commander takes responsibility for taking down the circle. He or she will first call the Artificer and their crew to take down the quarters. The same crew members who raised the quarters will now take the quarters down.

North Quarter Altar

The member extinguishes the candle, saying:

> Gods and spirits of the north. We thank you for leaving your factories, your foundries, and your deep earthen mines. Return to your realm if you must; remain in our realm if you wish.

East Quarter Altar

The member extinguishes the candle, saying:

> Gods and spirits of the east. We thank you for leaving your airships, your gaseous realms of hot air, helium, and hydrogen. Thank you for bringing your envelopes and your propellers, your lift machines, and your altimeters. Return to your realm if you must; remain in our realm if you wish.

South Quarter Altar

The member extinguishes the candle, saying:

> Gods and spirits of the south. We thank you for leaving your coal mines that light our fires and lift our ships, and your furnaces that melt our metals. Return to your realm if you must; remain in our realm if you wish.

West Quarter Altar

The member extinguishes the candle, saying:

> Gods and spirits of the west. We thank you for leaving your water that fills our tanks and your steam that drives our ships. Return to your frozen realm and misty clouds if you must; remain in our realm if you wish.

The Artificer dismisses his crew and reports to the Commander that the quarters are now down. The Commander thanks the Artificer and dismisses him or her.

The Commander then will call the Shipwright and ask:

Is the ship prepared to dock?

The Shipwright answers that the ship is safe to dock, and the Shipwright then returns to his station among the assemblage.

At this point the Commander reports to the Captain that the circle is ready to be taken down. Taking the key from the directional gear on the altar, the Captain walks clockwise from north and says:

> The gears have stopped and the steam is vented. We end this circle that we may land safely and rejoin our brethren on the ground. This circle is open but we are always safe within the aether. Steam down.

The members of the circle perform the Steam Down salute and say in unison:

Steam down.

The Captain then watches as the rest of the crew leave the circle area. Once the Captain is the last member in the circle area, he or she will leave.

Dismantling the Ship

All items on the main altar and quarter altars are removed and stored in the reverse order that they are placed during assembly.

The Short Circle

There will be times you wish to do a ritual or spell that calls for a circle. Not all spells need a circle, and calling and casting a full circle is oftentimes more cumbersome than you may wish to get into. There are times when a ritual or spell just needs that extra push to get it over the top, though. For those cases you may use the short circle. This is an abbreviated circle that is as powerful in some respects as a full circle, but you can do it alone and in less time.

On the main altar place the directional gear, the compass, and whatever other tools you may need for the spell. If you are using a wand to call and cast, then you may omit the spike and the rigging knife. If you have a spell that needs goggles then include them, but if they are not part of the spell then leave them off. You will notice that the altar looks quite barren sometimes, but you are laying out only what is essential to make the spell work. Also, you may place the tools wherever you need them to be handy. If you are left-handed then place the wand on the left of the compass, which is still in the center for orientation. Make the reaches short and easy. This is not an altar that is highly organized.

> *The Short Circle is a quick way of getting the job done.*

There are also no quarter altars in casting the short circle. Once you orient the directional gear to north, cast your circle without candles or anything else. Invite the gods and spirits to your circle and then begin as your spell instructs. When you have concluded the spell, take down the circle as easily as you cast it. We take the procedures very seriously in the short circle, but we do not dwell on ceremony.

The Short Circle is a quick way of getting the job done. When I was growing up I was raised Irish Catholic. Instead of going to high mass on Sunday my parents would take me to the Saturday mass that was only thirty-five minutes long. We were told it was the same mass but shorter. The Short Circle is similar to that. It's when you want the added power of a Circle but either don't have the time or inclination to cast a full circle. I guess you could think of the two as Circle and Circle Lite.

6

RITUALS AND OTHER CIRCLES

If I could create an ideal world, it would be an England with the fire of the Elizabethans, the correct taste of the Georgians, and the refinement and pure ideals of the Victorians.

—H. P. LOVECRAFT

In Steampunk Magic we have both rituals and circles. We discussed the main circle in the last chapter, but there are other circles that we use to celebrate important dates in our system. There are also important points in the lives of the crew members that make rituals essential. I have divided this chapter into rituals first and circles second since there are more rituals and they begin with birth and progress throughout all stages of life.

Rituals

Ritual for the Birth of a Child

The birth of a child is a joyous and memorable occasion, and the birth of a child within the magical community is especially joyous, since we are adding another special life to our numbers. When a crew member gives birth, the crew meets the new child and welcomes them to the world of Steampunk Magic. Whether the child grows up to become a member of the crew at adolescence or chooses a different path is not for this ritual. This ritual is to present the child to the entire crew and the entire crew to the child.

> *The birth of a child within the magical community is especially joyous.*

As soon as the parents feel that the child is safe to travel and be around many different individuals, a circle is called. This circle may coincide with another pre-planned ritual or circle, and the welcoming ritual may be wrapped into the circle.

At the proper time in the ritual the Captain calls the parents and child to the main altar. Even if only one parent is a member of the crew both parents may be present. Friends and family of the child may also be invited to this circle if the parents desire.

The Captain begins by saying:

> We are here tonight to welcome a new member to the world of Steampunk Magic. (Name each parent) has brought before us (child's name) to be presented as a

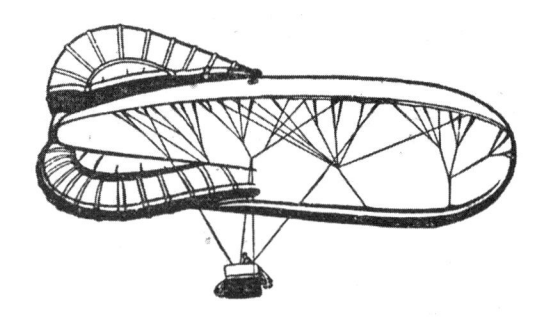

new young member. Whether this fine child will join our ship at the proper time or strike out on (his/her) own is not our decision to make. At this time we are gathered to present their first talisman to protect (him/her) as (he/she) travels through the aether and life.

The parents present the talisman that they made for their child. They either lay it on top of the child or attach it with a safety pin to the child's clothing and say:

> We present to you and the world (child's name). We ask the gods and spirits to watch over (him/her) when we are not able to. We ask the gods and spirits to be present when (he/she) is in need of guidance and direction. We charge the airship to be present whenever (he/she) needs information, spiritual direction, or assistance. We do this in the name of (airship's name).

The parents take the child around to each crew member, who then has the opportunity to whisper a blessing, piece of advice, or just good wishes to the child. At this time the crew members may also present the child with a small gift or talisman for good luck or success in the coming years.

Once all the crew have met the child the Captain says:

We are blessed by the gods and spirits to have this opportunity. May the gods and spirits remain with this child for as long as necessary. I charge the crew and those in attendance to watch over this child and assist this child as (he/she) grows to adulthood.

The Captain then thanks each parent, and the parents take their place in the general assemblage. If this is the only reason for the ritual then the Captain takes down the circle and the ritual is concluded. If there is more to do then the rest of the circle business continues.

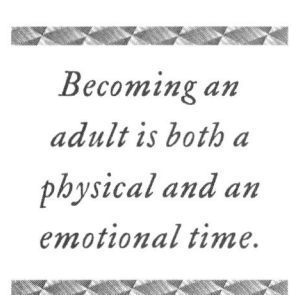

Becoming an adult is both a physical and an emotional time.

After the ritual is concluded there may be a small meal in celebration of the new birth. At this time crew members and friends of the ship can meet the new child and present gifts. After this ritual, the child may now be part of the circles and rituals if the parents and the crew so choose until the child comes of age at thirteen. At that point, the young adult must make a commitment to become a full member of the crew.

Coming of Age Ritual: Becoming an Adult

Becoming an adult is both a physical and an emotional time. Bodies change and functions change with them. Girls become women and boys become men; and no two individuals will reach that point at the same time. This ritual is for a child of a crew member who is at the stage of becoming an adult. Because the timing of becoming an adult and coming of age is not carved in stone, there is flexibility for when this ritual may be performed. As with accepting a new student, communication is everything. If the parents of the child, the child, and the airship all agree that the child is of adequate maturity to understand the nuances of Steampunk Magic and has proven that he or she is capable of conducting themselves in a safe, sane, consensual, and productive manner within the ship, then the time will be right for this ritual.

At the chosen time the young adult and the parents request a circle for adulthood. The crew assembles at the next full moon and a circle is cast. The Captain calls the young adult to the main altar along with the parents and says:

> (Name) has achieved adulthood. (He/She) is now ready to become responsible for (his/her) actions and will be treated as an adult from this time forward. An adult should never be unprepared for what life has in store for them. An adult should know safety and security through their own actions. An adult takes responsibility for what they do and what they say. Are you prepared to be an adult?

The young adult looks at the Captain and says:

I am prepared to be responsible for my words and deeds. I shall always honor my parents, live with them as I may, protect them and myself as I must, and travel this world as an adult. I take this oath knowing that from this day forward whatever I do is on me and I shall reap both the successes and failures with a clear head and an honest heart.

The parents present the young adult with a rigging knife, blade pointed down, and say:

We gift you this rigging knife that you may be prepared for life's uncertainties. Raise the blade only when necessary and thrust only when there is no other option. With this knife we cut the cord that ties the child to us and we welcome the (man/woman) that stands before us.

The Captain says:

You are now an adult with adult responsibilities and adult consequences. While you are always a child to your parents, as your children shall always be to you, you are now prepared for what lies ahead. May the gods and spirits watch over you during your life and guide you when you need it.

The new adult now turns to face the crew. The Captain says:

At the chosen time the young adult and the parents request a circle for adulthood.

I present you with (name), who is now a (man/woman) in our eyes. (He/She) shall be treated as such by those assembled here. However, remember that we are all someone's children, and at times we all need guidance and leadership. I charge the crew to offer that guidance and leadership if requested. Steam Up.

The crew gives the Steam Up salute. Once this portion of the ritual is completed, the circle is taken down and a celebration follows.

Coming of Age Ritual: Joining the Ship

This ritual is different from the young adult coming of age ritual, which may happen during a range of time. This ritual should be performed at a single specific time during the child's life.

Adolescence. A time when nothing makes sense. Voices change, body functions change, feelings change, and interests are . . . well, we'll leave it at that. The young child who yesterday was playing with models and dolls, pushing toy trucks, and riding bikes now wants to join the airship and be a crew member. They are old enough to understand ritual and the concept of magic as a system and not just as a plot development in a book of fiction. They are teenagers and they have a desire that should not be quelled. However, they are also still under the age of consent and so must have parental consent to join the ship. This is especially true if neither parent is a member of the ship or of the Steampunk Magical System.

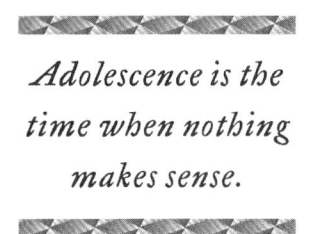

Adolescence is the time when nothing makes sense.

This ritual takes place on or soon after the youth's thirteenth birthday. If the youth wishes to join the crew of the ship, then at that time they are initiated into the system and welcomed aboard. The initiation ritual may be performed as part of a birthday ritual, or you may cast a new circle and perform the ritual specifically for this occasion. If you choose to combine this ritual with the birthday ritual then make certain that the youth and the crew understand that this is for the youth only and if there are other crew members with birthdays another ritual should be performed. This is a special moment, and the importance of the ritual cannot be downplayed. This ritual is also not to be confused with the previous coming of age ritual, which is a physical transformation ritual and does not involve the young adult becoming a crew member.

Once the circle is cast, the youth is called to the center of the circle. If the youth's parents are members of the crew then they are called next. It is customary that one or both of the child's parents act as sponsors, although it is not unusual for another member of the crew to take on that responsibility.

The Captain and Commander preside over the ritual with the entire crew looking on.

The coming of age ritual takes place on or soon after the youth's 13th birthday.

The Captain says:

> We have before us (name) who today is a (man/woman) and wishes to join our ranks as a crewmember of (ship name). Who speaks in support of this individual?

At this time either one or both of the parents or the sponsor says:

> I speak for (name).

The Captain says:

> Is this youth prepared to be taught the ways of Steampunk Magic and take (his/her) position in the circle and within our crew?

The parents/sponsor reply:

Yes, (he/she) is prepared.

The Captain says to the youth:

Are you prepared to be taught the ways of Steampunk Magic and take your position in the circle and within our crew?

The youth says:

I am.

The Captain then says to the youth:

Do you, (name), freely join this circle and this crew to be bound by the laws and oaths of our ship and by the principles of the Steampunk Magic System?

The youth says:

Yes, I do.

At this point the Commander says:

Who sponsors this new crew member?

The parents/sponsor replies:

I accept that responsibility.

The Captain looks out to the crew and says:

Is there anyone present who rejects this individual as a member of our crew or rejects (name of sponsor) as the sponsor of this new member?

At this time anyone who objects to the youth would state their objections and a majority vote would be taken. Voting majorities and those who may override voting are at the discretion of each individual ship. It is very unusual for there to be an objection. By this time, the youth has been integrated through the years into the workings of the ship and the system.

The Captain turns to the crew and places his/her right hand on the youth's right shoulder. The Captain then turns the youth to face the crew and says:

I present you (name), who by (his/her) own words and deeds has shown and spoken that (he/she) is ready to join our ranks as an enlisted crew member. Each of you is tasked to teach this new member what is necessary to become a valued member of this crew and to take their place as we travel through the aether. All those in favor of admitting this member to the crew say aye.

The crew responds with aye. At that point the Captain turns the youth back around with his right hand on the youth's right shoulder, looks the youth in the eyes, and says:

It is the wish of the crew that you be admitted to the ranks of enlisted members.

The Captain presents the new member with a small crystal of the Captain's choice.

This crystal is your beginning into the mysteries of Steampunk Magic. Keep this as your first talisman, and if you so choose begin crafting your tools from this meager beginning.

The new member takes the crystal. The Captain turns the member back around to face the entire crew and says:

I present you with (name), the newest member of our crew. Steam up and forward.

The Captain performs the Steam Up salute. The rest of the crew replies:

Steam up and forward.

Once that portion of the ritual is completed, the new member joins the rest of the crew and the circle is taken down. At this point during the post-ritual celebrating crew members may give the new member tools, books, or other small gifts as a welcome.

Ritual to Join the Airship Crew as an Adult

We all want to be wanted by others. We also all want to be members of the "cool" crowd or the in crowd, though we might not say it. The airship is oftentimes where you make your closest friends, even closer at times than your family. These are the people who share your hopes, dreams, and wishes for a better tomorrow. These are also the people other people want to be like and to join in with. Therefore you will eventually and on a rather regular basis be asked by individuals to join your ranks.

> *The airship is oftentimes where you make your closest friends.*

How you determine who you wish on your crew is up to your crew and your staff. There is often a vetting process in many paths and the individual is asked to sit in on a few open rituals or circles to be observed and to observe. This is a two-way acceptance. They are looking at you as much as you are looking at them, and it is imperative that everyone agree before oaths are exchanged.

The acceptance ritual is relatively simple. Before the ritual is scheduled to take place, the sponsor of the new member approaches the crew and recounts why the individual wants to join the ship and why the sponsor believes that the acceptance of the member would be a good idea. Then each member of the crew has a chance to say anything that is pertinent to the situation, positive or negative. They may recount observations from past circles or past meetings. If there is a written test to be a crew member, then the test is discussed and scores are evaluated. Finally, a decision is reached, and if its in the prospective member's favor, a ritual is scheduled and the sponsor prepares a talisman for the new initiate.

Your crew are the people who share your hopes, dreams, and wishes for a better tomorrow.

At the next new moon the crew is assembled and the circle is cast. The sponsor brings in the new member and presents him or her to the airship crew.

Facing the crew, the sponsor says:

> I submit this member for acceptance to our crew. I have known (name) for (number of months/years) and have found (him/her) to be an honorable and worthy member of our society. I support this member and will be responsible for (him/her) for the required one year and a day as our ship requires.

The Captain then says:

> Do you, (name), accept the rules and restrictions of our ship? Will you protect our ship and its secrets above all else and guard against those that would damage our good name and crew?

The individual says:

Yes.

Captain then says:

Is there anyone on the crew who objects to this membership?

At this point there should be no objection; all issues with the new member should have been worked out previously. When no one objects the Captain continues:

Who has the talisman for this new member?

The Commander takes the talisman from the main altar and hands it to the sponsor.

The sponsor says:

Accept this as your talisman of membership. When you are ready to create your own, you may place this on your altar. Should you ever decide to leave the ship, this will be returned. Do you accept this?

The new member says:

I do.

The Captain then says:

(Name), you have accepted the talisman as presented by your sponsor. You have by your words and actions proven that you are fit to hold a position in our crew and on our ship. Look to your feet.

The new member looks down to see the airship rigging knife placed across the path between himself and the Captain.

Replace the knife and join us, or turn and leave now. This is your final choice warning.

The new member picks up the rigging knife and places it back on the altar where it belongs. The Captain then turns to the assemblage:

(Name) has joined our ranks. (He/She) has wielded our weapon in defense of the ship and by that act has shown (his/her) willingness to serve the membership. I now present our newest member.

There is much cheering.

Take your place next to your sponsor and try to stay out of trouble for a year and a day.

The Captain continues to address the crew.

We are prepared to fly high and far into the aether. But tonight we feast.

The circle is taken down and there is a celebration for the new member. At this time each crew member may give gifts to the new member and words of advice. The sponsor is responsible for the new member for the probationary period of the next 366 days. After that, the member is officially made a senior member of the crew.

Ritual to Initiate a Senior Crew Member

In many pagan traditions there is a rule for a year and a day. Many couples that meet and wish to marry or handfast often wait a year and a day before doing so, and many handfastings are committed for a year and a day before reassessing the relationship. In Steampunk Magic the year and a day tradition is also taken seriously. Why, you may ask? Because it allows those who may have chosen unwisely the option to change their minds. Call it a sort of buyer's remorse.

The year and a day gives everyone in the ship a chance to evaluate each other.

In this case, a year and a day tradition is applicable to joining the crew. Whether you have come of age and joined the crew of your airship or you have petitioned and been accepted to a new ship, there is a trial period of a year and a day before the final oath to the ship is given and received.

At the first available circle after a member has reached their year and a day mark aboard ship, the Captain will call the member and their sponsor (the original sponsor if possible, or a replacement if the original sponsor is no longer there) to the main altar in front of the crew. The Captain addresses the member and the rest of the crew in total.

> It has been a year and a day since (name) has joined our crew. It is now time to grant seniority to this member and bestow full rights and privileges. Be there anyone aboard who finds this individual unworthy of our ranks?

There should be no objections at this point. Good leadership and courtesy would dictate that by the time the individual is up for full membership to the crew, all reservations and problems would have either been resolved or the member would have been asked to leave.

The Captain waits a few moments, and when no one objects says:

> Finding no objection to this member we (name of the ship) grant full rights to (name). (Name of sponsor), you may now return to your post. You have done well with this recruit and have earned all our gratitude.

The sponsor returns to his place in the crew. The Captain then turns to the member:

> I present you with Mr. (last name). Please take your place with the crew.

(In naval ranks, all members are considered Mr. if they are officers. In our ship we consider all senior members officers of the crew just from a point of view of respect. Other ships may vary on this.)

Although this is a very important ritual the length of the ritual is quite short. The crew member has been with you for over a year and during that time has worked, played, and eaten with you on many occasions. This is the final recognition of the situation.

Handfasting Ritual

Human beings are social animals. Although some of us may choose to be alone during our lives and in many circumstances are alone for long stretches of time we more than often find a mate, or if you wish wife/husband, partner, spouse, and become a couple in a more permanent relationship. In the wiccan and pagan traditions this is called handfasting, and Steampunk Magic follows this tradition. The handfasting ceremony is held with as much pomp and flair as the couple and those close to them choose.

> *Steampunk Magic does not limit a couple to being a traditional binary system.*

Those of us following Steampunk Magic does not limit a couple to being a traditional binary system of classification of husband and wife, though that may be applicable in a lot of cases. Therefore, in this ritual you have two individuals who have chosen to be joined in a union for the purpose of love and companionship. This ritual may be combined with a monthly ritual or another ceremony; however, since the celebration is so serious and long lasting, we recommend that this ceremony be held specifically for the reason of the handfasting.

Before the ritual is scheduled, the couple will approach the Captain and tell them they would like to have a handfasting ceremony. They will then choose matching items they would like to exchange during the ceremony. The couple may exchange any number of types of accoutrements as part of this ritual—rings, lapel pins, necklaces, stones, or whatever else has significance for them.

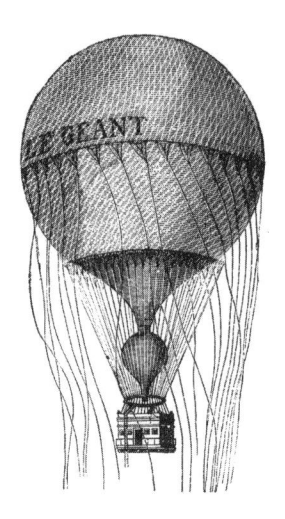

Once the circle is cast, the couple joins the Captain and the Commander at the center of the circle before the main altar. This is a ritual where all members of the crew dress accordingly. During monthly rituals and other coming of age and birth rituals members may choose whatever is appropriate for the weather, time of year, etc. This ritual, however, will bring out the best dress available to everyone. This ceremony should not be a cause for stress if you have only a few pieces of ritual garb and they are not formal

In a handfasting ritual the couple may exchange whatever has significance for them.

pieces. Dress as you will but at least make certain the clothing is neat, clean, and pressed.

The Captain begins by saying:

> We are gathered here on this day to join (name) and (name) together. They have each approached me and requested to be handfasted in the tradition of our ship. They have indicated that (items) shall be exchanged for this ceremony. It is a wondrous and perilous journey that we partake in our life. They have chosen to join forces and travel the roads and airs together out of love and companionship. They have chosen to do this after much consultation and visioning, and I believe they are ready to become a couple under the watchful eyes of this crew and to the world at large.

The Captain takes each of the partner's left hands in his/hers. The Captain then looks at the first partner and says:

> Repeat after me. I, (name), take you, (name), to be my partner, my protector, and my anchor. I agree to carry your burdens when necessary and to share your burdens when required. I will fly through weather fair and foul as the gods and spirits may choose for as long as we remain together.

The first partner repeats the vow.

The Captain then repeats the vows with the second partner.

At this point, the couple may exchange additional vows privately to each other or they may address the crew publicly. This is each person's chance to profess his or her personal love or promise for the future.

Rituals and Other Circles

Once that is completed, the Captain releases the couple's hands and says:

Walk with me.

The Captain leads the couple to the north quarter altar. There, he presents the couple with a piece of coal and says:

> Here you have fuel for your journey. May this and other pieces always be there for you, and if not then you have each other to gather more.

Next, the Captain leads the couple to the east altar and presents them with a balloon full of air. The captain says:

> Here is air. You now have the substance to lift you on your journeys. May they be safe and obstacle-free.

The Captain then takes the couple to the south altar and hands them a box of matches. He says:

> With this fire you may light your fuel to lift your ship in life. May you use this fire wisely. For as other things in life, fire may be a great boon or a cosmic destroyer.

Finally, the Captain leads the couple to the west altar and gives them a container of water, saying:

> You now have water for steam. The four elements are now in your hands to travel the world as one. Fly free and land well.

The Captain and the couple return to the main altar.

The Commander then takes two feathers from the main altar and gives one to each partner. The Commander says:

> With this feather your may fly on your own if you so choose. A handfasting is responsibility unbound. Should either of you feel that the flight is unsuited for you after consultation with those you hold in good stead, give this feather to the other and fly. You each have power over your own life and your own destiny.

The couple face the crew, and the Captain says:

> It is a great step to accept another in your life. You have each taken that step and bound yourself to the other for fair and foul. By the power granted me as Captain of this airship I present (name) and (name) as a recognized couple with all the privileges and responsibilities of any other handfasted couple.

The Captain points to a small container of boiling water casting steam by the entrance of the circle. The Captain holds his arm out toward the opening and says:

> You entered this circle as two equal yet separate individuals. Now go through the steam of the aether as a couple in love and companionship. Steam up and be well.

As the couple leaves the circle, the crew shouts:

> Steam up and be well!

At this point the circle is taken down and the celebration begins with the giving of gifts, food, drink, and music. If the Captain is a legally recognized justice of the peace or is licensed to perform marriages in the state, and the couple would like to be married in the eyes of the state, the Captain would sign the required documents and the couple would file them with the proper government agency.

Ritual for the Release of a Crew Member

I met a United States Air Force officer once when I was temporarily stationed in Omaha, Nebraska. He was a major on the list for promotion to lieutenant colonel. We were talking about being transferred often in the Army. I moved every year for a long time due to my specialty. He said that when he first received his commission, he was told to buy a house near a good school the day after he arrived in Omaha. He didn't even have a girlfriend, but he did as he was told. I asked him how that worked out, and he said his youngest daughter will graduate next year from the high school down the block. He had been in the same house for twenty-two years.

Not everyone is fortunate enough to be able to put down roots and stay put. Whether by circumstance or by choice, others travel and see the world. Eventually you are going to have a crew member who wishes to leave the crew due to work, travel, disinterest, or other personal reasons. While there will be sadness for the loss of a crew member, there should still be a celebration of a new journey ahead. This should be a joyous celebration for the sake of the crew member leaving. Even though there will be many tears and pains of losing a good friend, at least the member is alive and well and going somewhere else; or at least we may hope that is the case.

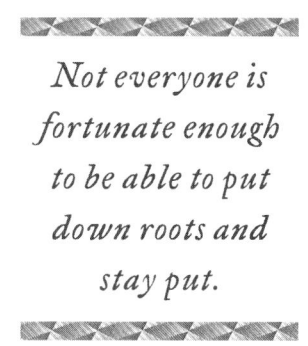

> *Not everyone is fortunate enough to be able to put down roots and stay put.*

Once the circle is cast, the crew member who is leaving addresses the crew. There are a few options for how this ritual can proceed. The crew member may explain why he is leaving, or he may keep that information to himself. He may also choose to have others speak about his time on the ship, or he may choose to leave in a rather quiet manner. At any rate the crew member has the option to design his and the other's involvement since it is his time to say goodbye.

Once the crew member has finished addressing the crew he turns to the Captain. At that time the Captain accepts any talisman that ties the crew member to the ship. This may be something that was given to him as a crew member or something that he used specifically for ritual as a member of the crew. Nothing personal will be requested from the departing member.

The Captain accepts the item and says:

> It is with a heavy heart that we release you from your service on our ship. Should you ever wish to return, [this (talisman) will be returned to you, and] you will once again take your rightful place aboard the ship.

If the crew member had nothing to give back, the line in brackets will be omitted.

Once the crew member has been released, he leaves the circle amidst cheers from the remaining crew. When the member is departed the Captain says:

> We have lost one of our own today. (He/She) is still among us in spirit and we look forward to someday

welcoming (him/her) back to us. Let us go and celebrate this next chapter in (name's) life.

The circle is taken down and the crew retires to bestow gifts on the member leaving.

Ritual for a Fallen Crew Member

We all die. This is a fact of life. Unfortunately we also all deal with death in our own ways and we grieve differently. Next to close family, your crew members can often be the closest friends and acquaintances you will ever have. They have studied with you, performed ritual and circle with you, and heard your innermost fears, joys, and wishes. These are the people who know more about you than maybe your own parents and children, and if your spouse does not practice Steampunk Magic they may know things even he or she does not know.

> *We all deal with death in our own ways and we grieve differently.*

I am a U.S. Army reserve officer. During my active duty time I spent six months as the officer in charge of a military burial detail in Southern California. During that time I spent many afternoons with the grieving spouse of a service member who had died. As the daughter of a World War II veteran, I also oversaw the burial of my father when he passed away. I was struck by the fact that the ritual of burial does not take into account the ritual of release. The family and friends grieve, and sometimes they have a memorial service before or after the burial, but most of the time they eat, drink, and talk but never address the one who has passed away.

This ritual is performed at a full moon with the entire airship present. If possible the talisman of the fallen member is placed on the altar that's most appropriate. For example, if the talisman is a key with a crystal then it may be placed at north or south. If the piece is a stone it will go at north, and so on.

> *The fallen crew member ritual is performed at a full moon with the entire airship present.*

After the circle is cast, light a coal fire in the heavy brazier. Get the fire as hot as possible. You want the inner coals to be glowing, almost white-hot.

The Captain takes the talisman in a pair of tongs or a long-handled pair of pliers and carefully places it in the very center of the brazier. As the Captain removes the tongs from the fire, he says:

> We are forged in the fires of the earth and buoyed up by the aether to glow in this world. We now say goodbye to (person's name), who passed away as a member of this crew. We give (name) permission to leave this physical space if (he/she) wishes to rise into the aether. As (his/her) talisman returns its energy to the void, let us remember (name) fondly and know that we shall all miss (him/her) but will keep (him/her) in our hearts.

At this point, each member of the airship tells stories or anecdotes about the deceased. The crew should be keeping the fire as hot as possible throughout this time. At the end of the storytelling, let the fire burn out.

Once the coals are cold and powdered collect all the ash along with the metals and stones of the talisman.

Take down the circle.

With as many members as possible, take the ashes and other pieces to a source of running water and throw them in, saying:

> We all come from water and to water we return. Sail well and fly free.

The ritual is now concluded.

Circles

The Victoria Circles

We don't have a deity in Steampunk Magic. However, that does not mean we don't have circles and rituals that mention or revolve around Victorian individuals. In our case there are two specific rituals, and they are bound by the birth and death of

Victoria herself. For lack of a better title I have them listed simply as the Victoria Circles. You may choose to refer to them as you wish when you begin practicing Steampunk Magic.

Without Queen Victoria there would be no steampunk, and no Steampunk Magic. Victoria was the beginning and end of the Victorian era, and we pay homage to her in two circles designed for birth and death.

Birth Circle
The birth circle takes place on May 24, Victoria's birthday. During this circle the attendees will look forward to their year ahead and consider how they may achieve their goals and aspirations. It is a time of celebration, hope, and joy.

To prepare for the birth circle each member of the airship brings fresh fruits and vegetables. Nothing is cooked, though dressings and sauces may be purchased locally. You will want dishes of some of the following. These may be spread out on a sideboard for consumption after the circle.

- fresh carrots
- scallions
- waxed rutabagas

- cucumbers
- turnips
- cabbage
- salads

There should also be a variety of fruits, such as

- strawberries
- blueberries
- apples
- oranges
- grapes
- pineapples
- apple, grape, and cranberry juice
- sides of dressings, oils, and vinegars for dipping

After the circle has been cast, gather around the altar and on small pieces of parchment paper write down your wishes, hopes, and dreams for the year. Each member holds these papers close to their heart and concentrates on achieving those things they most desire. During this time the Captain gives a brief background of the reason for the circle and the intended outcome. Each airship will be different, but here is a sample:

> We are gathered here tonight to celebrate another year. We give thanks to Victoria, Queen of the Realm, for her birth and ascension to the throne of England and the British Empire. Tonight we look forward to what our year will bring and how we may achieve that. Don your goggles and look into the aether. Through the mist and the smoke of the world we pierce the veil to the clear and endless space of pure air and endless stars. We sail clear and safely toward our destination of success, health, happiness, and whatever else you most desire this year. When you are ready to release your needs and desires to the aether, place your papers in the censer. Then say or think, "I release these desires to the aether to return to me positively."

Once everyone has released their papers to the aether, close the meditation by saying:

We have released our needs and wants to the aether for the year. It is time to act upon these requests. Remember nothing comes to you freely; you must work and labor for your rewards. As you leave this circle tonight dedicate yourself to achieving your goals. We will now open the circle.

Open the circle. Once the circle has been opened, all members of the airship will meet at the sideboard and feast on the fresh bounty of the spring.

Please remember to leave a small repast to the gods and spirits of the aether when the night is concluded. You may set out a small dish of fresh fruits and vegetables by the altar or if you have a specific statue or place in the yard for such, leave the dish there.

Death Circle
On January 22, Victoria passed away, and Edward became King of England. With his ascension the Edwardian era began, and the industrial and technological revolutions went into full swing with the popularity of gasoline, alternating current, diesel, and eventually atomic power. Wars were fought with great war machines of immense power and destruction, and the world would never again be the same.

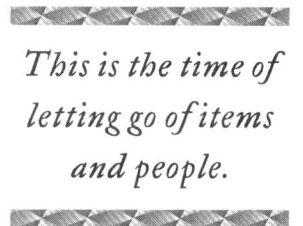

This is the time of letting go of items and people.

The death circle is a somber time of mourning and loss. The Queen is dead, as they say, long live the King. However, more than the Queen has passed through the veil; the entire era of Victoriana has gone as well. This is the time of letting go of items and people. We shall allow those we hold dear but have lost to safely pass into the aether.

To prepare for the death circle, airship members should bring cooked, pickled, or canned items. This is the middle of the winter, and most fresh foods will have been exhausted by now. That which is left in the larder are foods that have been prepared earlier and preserved for these harder times.

Possible options include:

- dried meats, such as jerky, dried beef, or salted hams
- salted fish, such as sardines, pickled herring, or oysters
- wrapped meats, such as pepperoni or salami
- cheeses
- canned vegetables, such as corn, carrots, potatoes, or beans—usually lima or green
- canned fruits, such as jams or jellies
- olives
- peppers
- pickles
- wine
- beer
- apple cider

After the circle is cast, the Captain or the designated individual instructs the members of the airship to sit either on blankets or chairs comfortably around the fire. The fire for this circle is a larger fire pit or an above ground fire. If you are letting go of an individual, then it would be appropriate to bring a small piece of cloth from that person's shirt, pants, or dress. If you are trying to let go of a habit, a memory, or something that is more ethereal, then bring a piece of wood that is flat on one side or a piece of parchment.

The Captain gives a brief background of the day and the ceremony. Here is a sample:

> We all mourn Victoria, Queen of England and the British Empire. May her memory live onward for eternity. As she passes through the aether, let us take this time to think about others we have lost this year.

> Have you experienced death? During this time let us cast off those memories and afflictions we have collected over the year. Let us remember those we have lost, but let us also remember that too many memories will cloud the voyage into the future. Do not forget those who have gone this year. Give those who have died

permission to leave us with their memory but without their energies.

Is there something you wish to lose but are bound to, as the airship is anchored to the earth? Habits, illnesses, personal disasters, or failures all may be released to the aether at this time to fade into the void. Store them away in your mind and let them trouble you no more.

The fire burns brightly in the night air. Don your goggles, see the smoke dissipate, rising ever higher until it disappears in the darkness. Throw off your shackles and your chains of despair, loss, and misery.

When you are ready, throw your pieces into the fire. As you do this, say or think, "I release you to the aether. Go willingly if you wish, or unwillingly if you must. I shall remember but no longer dwell on you."

When all have cast their pieces into the fire, let the fire burn out naturally. When the Captain is ready to close the circle, he says:

We have released our burdens to the aether. Go out into the world free of heavy thought or dark afflictions.

After the circle is closed the members feast on the last of the winter's bounty. Leave a dish for the gods and spirits by the altar or wherever you have designated.

The Birthday Circle

The day of your birth is often a time of great joy. You have turned eighteen, or twenty-one, or thirty, or some other age that is important to you. You have survived a major catastrophe or illness, you have gotten through a difficult time at work, or you have passed your classes at school.

Your birthday can also be a time of great upheaval. You may be anxious about getting older. You may feel as you approach whatever age you feel is a milestone that you are no longer able to fulfill your obligations.

I have never liked my birthdays. I was born on my parents' wedding anniversary, so my birthday was a secondary event. I joined the Army on my birthday and a year later exactly signed into Officer Candidate School. My birthday was also the birthday of the United States Army, and all the years I was an active duty soldier and officer I had to attend mandatory formations and social gatherings that kept me from taking the day off to enjoy it the way I wished. To add to my distress, my mother-in-law died on my birthday years later from a sudden heart attack.

The birthday circle is one of reflection and projection.

As I grew older I lamented what I had not yet done and every year I saw the time I had to accomplish something slip away. When I hit thirty I realized that getting older is a natural state of being. I had already outlived many of the soldiers I served with in the Army, and that saddened me greatly. I wrote the birthday circle that year, after I came back from Korea. I have since cleaned it up over the years so it has a better feel to it, but the intent is the same. Interestingly enough, now that I practice Steampunk Magic, I have found that my birthday coincides with National Steampunk Day. So at least I now have a positive celebration to enjoy.

The birthday circle is one of reflection and projection: Where have you been the past year? What have you accomplished? What kept you from finishing your goals? You also have a new year to look forward to. You are able to wipe the slate clean of what you did the past year and start again with new plans and new accomplishments. The birthday ritual is finally one of renewal. Scientists say that the entire body regenerates itself every seven years. Therefore, if you are over seven years old, you are regenerating something every year. This is the perfect ritual to begin again and welcome the new you. This ritual should be performed on your birthday if possible or as close to the actual day as you can manage.

You will need:

- birthday cards you have received from friends and family
- small slip of paper

- pen
- white candle
- lemongrass oil
- matches
- brazier

Begin with a short circle, since you will most likely be the only one performing this circle. Once circle is cast, dress the white candle with lemongrass oil and set it in a candleholder on the main altar at the south position. Dressing a candle is rubbing oil on all sides of the candle before lighting it. Take up a comfortable position in a chair or on the floor and light the candle.

Project what you wish to do or what you don't want to do in the future year.

Stare into the candle and reflect on what has come to pass this year. Take as long as you need to.

Continue staring into the candle as you project what you wish to do in the future year or what you don't want to do that you tried to end and failed at. When you are ready write on one side of the paper the things you wish to remove from your past year—the mistakes, the errors, and the memories that are no longer necessary. On the other side of the paper write down the things you wish to accomplish this coming year—finish a project, gain or lose weight, learn something new, whatever you may wish.

When you are ready to complete the ritual, hold the piece of paper over the flame of the candle until it catches on fire.

As you put the piece of paper in the brazier to burn out on the altar say:

> I have looked back. I have looked ahead. I know where I am and where I wish to be. That which is behind me makes me stronger. That which is ahead of me gives me direction. I am my own pilot and my own ship. I make my own future, thusly creating my own history.

When the paper has burned out you may extinguish the candle and use it for next year if there is any left. Then take down the circle. You are prepared for another year.

7

VISIONING AND DIVINATION

I do not think there is any thrill that can go through the human heart like that felt by the inventor as he sees some creation of the brain unfolding to success . . . such emotions make a man forget food, sleep, friends, love, everything.

—Nikola Tesla

The aether gives us life. It is, as we have been led to believe and have no reason to doubt, the air of the gods. By using the aether we may see what we are looking for. Visioning in Steampunk Magic allows us to peer into the aether unobstructed.

Preparing for Visioning

Concentration is paramount to good visioning. Without concentration your thoughts will stray and wander to the point of distraction. Therefore, the first stage of good visioning is finding a quiet and comfortable place to meditate.

The second stage of good visioning is to find a system or process that works for you. There is no one-size-fits-all approach to visioning. Each of us is unique, and each of us requires a visioning technique that is as unique as we are. I find myself falling asleep at any attempt to meditate or vision in a perfectly quiet room or setting. It doesn't matter if I just got out of bed after a full night's sleep—if I attempt to vision or meditate in a quiet or darkened room, I will be asleep almost immediately. Different techniques are included here for those who are like me; and for those who are fortunate enough to be able to concentrate and not fall asleep in a quiet, darkened room, there are options here for you, too.

The Elements and Visioning

There are four elements: earth, air, fire, and water; and a final fifth "element," the void, which is the absence of all other elements. Each element speaks to us in a different language and may be interpreted in many different ways. In Steampunk Magic, visioning the elements should be considered separately, as each has its own visioning style. Further, each element has its own specific areas that are applicable to the visioning.

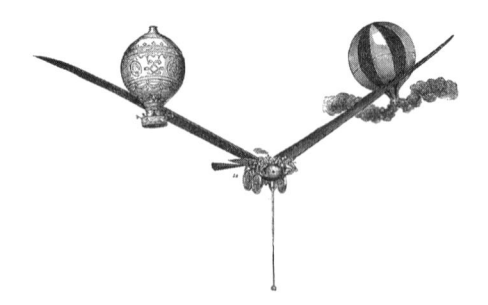

For:	Vision on:
Money, protection, binding, land advice	Earth
Birth, a new beginning, health, reconnections, past hurts, travel	Air and the sunrise of each new day that warms the air around us
Love, passion, romance, sex	Fire
Death; good-byes to people, animals, or situations	Water and the setting of the sun
Your spiritual path, other situations that are not applicable to another element or that involve multiple elements	The void

Earth

We draw strength from the earth. Deep in the earth it is cool and dark. No light penetrates the earth, and the magnetic lines are stronger the deeper you go. Each element has a strength and a weakness. Earth is as strong as the ground we stand on, since it *is* the ground we stand on. It is "rock solid," as some say, and we call the earth *terra firma* to indicate that the ground beneath us is not going anywhere too soon. However, earth can also be washed away by water or blown away by air; the strongest granite can be destroyed by a single drop of water repetitively striking the same point.

To vision on the earth element, procure a piece of hematite. Hematite is a magnetic ore that is representative of the northern clime. Find a comfortable position in a cool, quiet, and darkened space. Hold the hematite and see yourself deep in the earth or on the ground beneath the stars. Articulate in your mind your reason for the visioning. You may wish to review the attributes of hematite in *Cunningham's Encyclopedia of Crystal, Gem, & Metal Magic* and ground with the hematite as part of your visioning.

Air

Air moves all around us. We fly through the air, and from the air we enter the aether. Air has the strength to blow down houses or rip up the grasses we grow beneath our feet. Oxygen provides power to our lungs as the currents provide direction to our sails. Air may be harnessed, though, and made to work for us. We heat air to lift our ships and direct air to power our windmills. We may redirect air to protect our houses and our crops, and when necessary we may divert air with the heat of fire.

> *Each element speaks to us in a different language and may be interpreted in different ways.*

This visioning is best performed early in the morning when the sun, another eastern element, is rising. Find a comfortable position. In a dimly lit space with a small fan blowing into your face, articulate in your mind your reason for the visioning. If you have the time, try to find a five-minute audio file of an airship propeller engine to vision to. In lieu of an airship engine, you can also look for a heavy industrial propeller engine from an airplane. My friend Braxton Ballew of Valentine Wolfe came up with a great five-minute loop of an engine that works perfectly. Start the recording at the beginning of the visioning, and when the track is done you know you have reached five minutes. The link is available at *www.valentinewolfe.com*.

Fire

Fire provides steam to run our machines and heats air to lift our ships. Fire lights our way with the lamp in the aether. Fire burns everything near it. We heat our water to provide steam with fire. Fire forges our metals and warms our houses; it cooks our food and sterilizes our instruments. But fire is contained by earth. A hole in the ground will contain a fire just by being a hole in the ground. Without air, fire won't burn and if doused by water fire will extinguish. Fire is powerful and fragile at the same time.

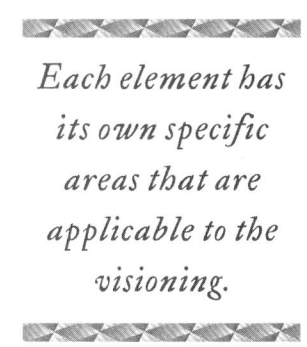

> *Each element has its own specific areas that are applicable to the visioning.*

If possible find a comfortable, quiet position outside beneath the stars. With the lamp as your guide, stare into the flickering light and articulate in your mind your reason for the visioning.

Water

We are closest to our ancestors through water. We are surrounded in the womb by water, and surrounded by water we shall vision. Water gives us life. We are primarily water with some other important elements thrown in. We must consume water as much as we must breathe air. Water cleanses us, nourishes us, and provides steam for our ships. We swim in water and watch the rainbows created after water falls as rain. Water will also drown you. Too much water and you will die. The force of water can destroy entire cities as tsunamis, and frozen water as ice and snow will crush even the strongest earthen structure. Very few organisms can live in frozen water.

In a bathtub or small pool of warm water, light a small blue candle and set it at the foot of the tub. As the sun is setting allow the room to darken naturally while articulating in your mind your reason for the visioning.

The Void

The void is the absence of all elements. Think of the void as both white and black in the color and value spectrums: white is the absence of all color, while black is the inclusion of all colors. The void is similar to this. It is the absence of all elements, where there is nothing but the questioner and the question, and it is the inclusion of all elements, since it may be used when you are uncertain of where else to go.

> *In Steampunk Magic visioning the elements should be considered separately.*

There is nothing in the void, so find an empty, quiet space with no distractions. There is no light in the void, so the space should be black. Release all your thoughts and physical feelings. Make yourself as comfortable as you can so there is minimal contact with anything. Once you are in a total feeling of emptiness, articulate in your mind the reason for the visioning.

Divination

Tarot is an age-old form of divination that is still viable. Although any tarot deck may be used for reading, I love the new Steampunk Tarot deck by Barbara Moore and Aly Fell. It has amazing graphics and descriptions of the cards in a large book that is also well illustrated. To say that the steampunk graphics had nothing to do with my choice of deck would be dishonest, and really any deck will do, but . . .

While most think of a tarot reading as a linear progression of cards, moving from one timeframe to another, in Steampunk Magic I envision the tarot spread as a navigational chart. You may also think of it as a map to a future that you have the power to change incrementally if you so wish. Either way you look at it, tarot is a way to travel your near future with the obstacles and the smooth sections identified.

The Six-Tooth Gear Spread

The Six-Tooth Gear Spread is unique to Steampunk Magic (see figure 23). Unlike many other tarot spreads, there is a far past and a near past in the card layout. The far past looks at the deepest roots of the question or issue at hand and the near past allows the reader to see how the question or issue has improved, worsened, or maintained over time. The present is, as in other spreads, the current situation as it appears. The spread also has hopes and fears thus assisting the reader in seeing the present in a clear and finely-tuned manner. Finally, the reader is given the future as it will turn out if the course is held.

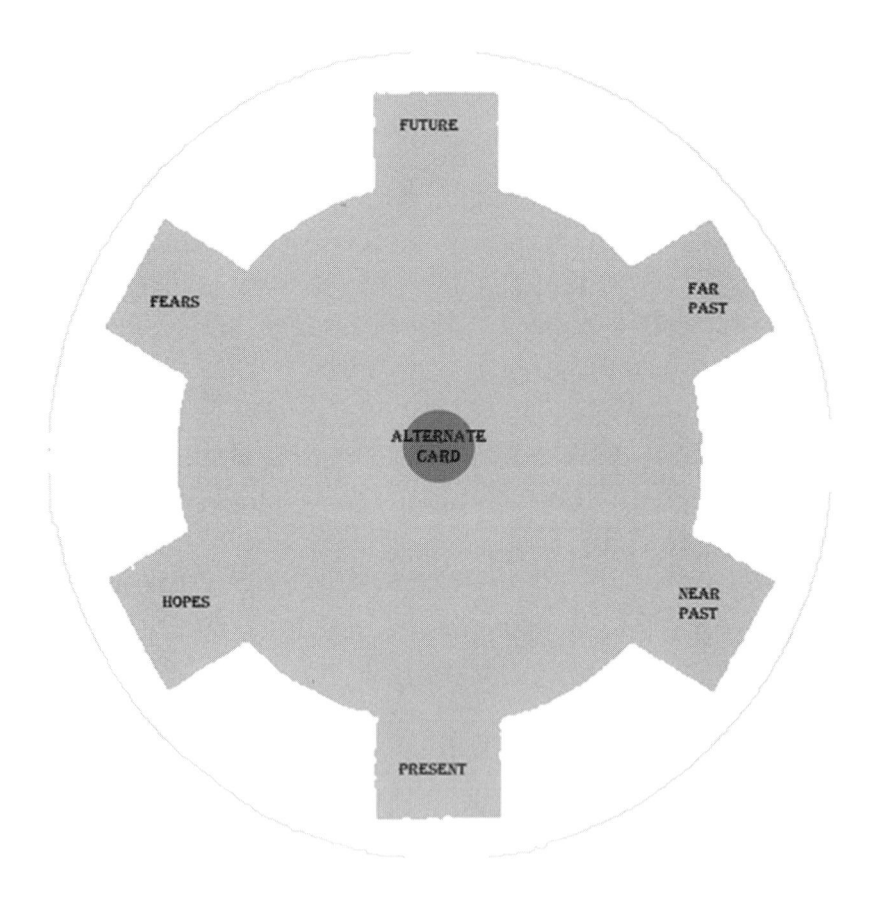

Figure 23. The Six-Tooth Gear Spread.

Once you have shuffled the cards, you may either draw the cards from the top of the deck or cut the deck and draw from the center. Lay all six cards face down on the spread, starting with the Far Past on the upper right and working in a clockwise manner until you reach the Future. Do not draw the Alternative Card in the center yet.

Let's look at each section and see what is different about this spread from all the others.

The 6 tooth gear spread gives you a deep past look at the core of the question.

The Far Past

The Far Past sets the basis for all actions that have come since. The Far Past is considered to have happened more than half your current age ago. It is the first card of the spread that is read, and it alerts the reader to the situations that ultimately created the question. The Far Past is oftentimes difficult to remember, sometimes clouded in guilt, shame, joy, or regret, and possibly it is even lost to the questioner. This card is paramount to understanding how the questioner arrived at their current location and should be considered for some time before continuing through the other cards of the spread.

The Near Past

The Near Past is no more than a year ago and more likely is only a few weeks or days past. This is the immediate cause of the question and where changes may be most critical. This card shows the tipping point that put the questioner where he or she currently is. The Near Past is oftentimes raw and open with

Visioning and Divination

emotions that may cloud the actual occurrence. Unlike the Far Past, the Near Past is too fresh. For this card the key is not to remember what happened but to be a fair witness to the facts that occurred.

In Robert A. Heinlein's book *Stranger in a Strange Land*, Michael Valentine Smith is hosted by Judge Jubal Harshaw. The Fair Witness, Anne, is asked what color Judge Harshaw's house is. Anne reports that the side of the house that she can see is white. A Fair Witness makes no attempt to assume or extrapolate what they cannot see; they only report what they actually know to be true from direct observation. You the questioner must be a Fair Witness to the near past. Look hard at the card, concentrate on the past activities that the card represents, and realize that the truth is most important to the outcome.

The fair witness view point gives you an objective look at the past.

The Present

The present is now. This is where the questioner is at this exact moment. It is important to remember that once the present card is turned, the present is frozen in time. It will become the near past once the spread is concluded, but for this one instant the present is just that—moving neither forward nor backward on the temporal continuum.

Again the questioner must remain objective to the details of the present. He or she must look at the current situation and reflect on whether they see the situation as it actually is or how they interpret it to be. This is another card that is important to the outcome of the spread since it shows all that is in the questioner's immediate sphere.

Hopes

We all have hopes, and we dream of better situations. Our hopes are what keep us moving forward. This card shows what the reader is truly hoping for, whether they are aware of it or not. Study this card. Reflect on what you want, what you dream of, and what you will aspire to. Does this card strike a chord in your psyche?

Finally, look into the aether. Close your eyes and imagine that you are sailing on the ship through the fine crisp air of the aether. What do you see beyond your bow?

Fears

The fears card is the opposite of the hopes card. It is what the reader subconsciously fears will come to pass. This card is essential in that it will show the reader the obstacles that are internal and external to the path of success. The fears card is to be taken very seriously in the final reading and in the final analysis of the entire spread.

As you looked ahead with the hope card, so must you look beneath you with the fears card. Close your eyes and look beneath the ship. Is your anchor attached to anything? Is there anything entangled in the ropes or lines of the ship? What cargo are you carrying that is too heavy or cumbersome to maneuver successfully?

Once you have identified all obstacles you must strike them off. Mentally push these fears off the side of your ship. Holding your rigging knife in your hand, mentally cut away that which is tangled in the nets, the ropes, and the lines. Free your ship of what is holding you back. If you cannot manage to free yourself of your fears and burdens at this time, mentally tag the thought, the concern, or the debilitation for future attention.

The Future

The future card is the most important card in the reading. I call this card the Richard Dawson card in honor of the most successful host of the long-running game show *Family Feud*. Just before the answer would be revealed Richard would always shout out, "survey says." The future card is that survey. This is what the future will be if something is not done to change the course of events.

Consider the future card your wake-up call. If you do nothing you will fly directly into whatever you have out there, and you know it. Therefore, look inward for your direction.

Take the information you now have and chart a new course if you feel you need to. Modify your course if that is your want, or stay the course if that suits your needs better. You have the inventory of your hopes. You have cut away as many of your fears as you can and you have identified those that are left. You see what is ahead of you if you stay your course. Therefore you need to take up your navigational charts and decide which way to go next. No matter what the outcome of this card, the choices and decisions you make are completely and uniquely yours. There is no one who can make these decisions for you.

> *The future card is the most important card in the reading.*

The Alternate Card

The alternate card is the axle card; it is placed in the center of the spread where the axle of the gear fits. This card is to be used as a fine-tuning of your reading. Do not put this card out unless you need it. But, if you are uncertain of your direction or your interpretation of the reading, then take the next card on the deck and place it over the axle hole on the gear. Read this card as you would any other and apply the nuances of that card to the final future card. Here you may see something you missed in the previous six cards. Do not make this card a regular card to your readings, though. This card is only for extreme situations when you have two almost identical choices to make in your future and one may be better or worse than the other.

Tarot readings by their nature are fluid. All tarot spreads are designed for the individuals and what works for the reader is the spread that should be used. This spread is but one of many; however, I believe that it meets the requirements for the reader in a manner never before offered. In conclusion, therefore, use what works for you.

8
SPELLS

Science has failed into many errors—errors which have been fortunate and useful rather than otherwise, for they have been the stepping-stones to truth.
—JULES VERNE, *A JOURNEY TO THE CENTRE OF THE EARTH*

Spells can be both beneficial and harmful, depending on the circumstances and the situation they are employed in. Spells may radiate out from the practitioner or radiate inward back to the practitioner. "Do as ye will, and harm none" is taken quite seriously in Steampunk Magic since the aether is a neutral space that is neither good nor evil. It is imperative that the practitioner be cautious of what they project their spells toward and that those they attempt to assist or deter are never named unless the individual concerned has granted them permission. Remember that whatever you put out into the aether will come back to you threefold.

The circle is another tool that you may call upon in your magical work. You have the option in spell work either to cast the circle for added clarity of purpose or not to cast the circle if you are experienced enough to be able to focus without it.

The spells presented here are a selection of workable spells and are not the only ones that may be called upon. Each Steampunk Magician is capable of writing his or her own spells. These are just the beginning.

Protection

Protection is an earth spell. You need the stability of the ground to protect you in your surroundings. In medieval times castles and immense earthworks were created out of the stones and dirt of the earth to protect those within from the forces of whatever was outside the perimeters. The structures are evident today as crumbling piles of rock or mounds of grasses in large fields, but they are still evident after millennia. That fact alone illustrates the force and perseverance of earth.

Personal Protection Against a Person or Persons

You will need:

- A small package of modeling clay—basic art clay is best, though play clay that comes in colors works as well
- Rigging knife
- Outdoor location where you can dig a small hole

Make a small sculpture of a person with the clay. This doll will be the representation of all those who are trying to do you harm now or have done you harm in the past. You do not need to be specific in your details since identifying a specific person against their will, even though they may be attempting harm to you, will only bring back upon you three times the damage you are trying to protect yourself against.

However, you should make the doll accurate enough to show two arms, two legs, a torso, and a head with a rudimentary face.

Spells may radiate out from the practitioner or radiate inward back to the practitioner.

Find a place that you can dig a hole. If you own your own home then at the farthest point from your front door is the best location. If you rent or live in a dormitory then a park or other open space is fine. With your rigging knife dig the hole large enough for the doll and at least twelve inches deep. Place the doll in the hole face down away from you. If you are at home, point the head away from your house. If you are in a public space, point the doll's head away from where you live. As you bury the doll, say:

> The Earth protects and tethers me in storm.
> The Earth is my mother and will keep me from harm.
> To the Earth I command this danger to melt away.
> And be gone from me beginning today.

The optimal time for this spell is during sunset, since you want to end something and the setting sun signals the end of another day. Also if the ground is damp or wet due to a recent rain, then the clay will dissolve faster and return the doll and its negative energies to the earth faster.

Protection of Your Home

Protecting your home casts a spell around your entire property to keep harm from affecting you and yours. The salt may be purchased at any grocery or convenience store and the salt crystals are often found at health food stores, or you may make your own. (See page 79.)

You will need:

- a large dish of salt
- four salt crystals
- spike
- rigging knife

Bury one of the salt crystals at each of the four corners of your property, starting with the northern-most corner. With your rigging knife dig a hole at least a foot deep. Place a salt crystal in the bottom of the hole and fill in the dirt. Drive your spike into the freshly dug earth where the first crystal was buried and say:

> Salt of the earth and salt of the sea,
> Salt that is essential and critical to me,
> I cast a spell around this space
> No evil shall enter, only good to this place.

Then sprinkle the dish of salt from corner to corner to create a barrier against anything advancing past that line. As you walk from the first corner to the second corner, cast the loose salt in an outward motion while staying within your property.

As you cast the salt, think of all negativity being banished to the aether where the gods may destroy it as they want.

Repeat the spell and visualization as you bury the second, third, and fourth salt crystals, casting the loose salt outward between points. As you close the circle around your property and return to the corner that you started at, drive the spike into the earth again and say:

> This barrier is now closed to all evil and those who practice it.

Attraction

There is a threefold rule in all magic that states that whatever you do will come back on you threefold. There is also a rede in magic that states "do as ye will, and harm none." Both of these are applicable to attraction spells. It is magically, morally, and ethically wrong to identify individuals for attraction. Television and movies are full of dolls and spells that bring individuals together with locks of hair and fingernails, but these are more suited to other religious traditions than to Steampunk Magic.

There is a threefold rule in all magic that states that whatever you do will come back on you threefold.

For attraction you want to bring someone into your life who is meant for you. You don't want to put constraints on the search. As a librarian I spend a lot of time with students and faculty discussing search parameters. Once the student realizes that the search verbiage is the most important part of the search, the book or article is much easier to find. An attraction spell is similar.

When I ran an occult supply store in Oklahoma I had a customer who wanted someone in her life. She would purchase candles and oils each week and repeat the process again and again. Finally we started talking about her search and how she was phrasing the spell. She told me she was looking for a tall, tanned, athletic man who would sweep her off her feet and they would travel the world together. It took me a few weeks to explain to her that such restrictive conditions were narrowing the possible choices to the point of almost zero. I suggested she might want to think about just asking for the person who was right for her and whom she was right for. I didn't see her again for a few weeks, and when I did she was with someone who was diametrically opposed to what she was originally asking for. That was twenty-five years ago, and as far as I know they are still together. It's all about the search.

> *There is also a rede in magic that states "do as ye will, and harm none."*

First Spell

In the early '90s I was at a pagan show in Texas selling oils and books. A woman came by my booth and picked up a vial of Dove's Blood Oil (a weaker version of Dragon's Blood Oil) and asked if it was from the real blood of doves. I was much younger then and had watched her go from one booth to the next trying to engage in philosophical discussions of her religion versus ours. When she asked the question I smiled, held up a vial of Dragon's Blood Oil, and said, "Yes ma'am, and this one's made from real dragons." She never realized I was kidding. Instead she just said "disgusting" and walked out of the hall. We never saw her again.

No dragons are harmed in the making of Dragon's Blood Oil. Dragon's Blood Oil comes from the sap of the Dragon Blood Tree found on the Socotra archipelago in the Indian Ocean. It is a very powerful oil and only a few drops are necessary for this spell. Since the trees are facing possible extinction please treat the oil with restraint and thank the tree for giving up its sap.

For this spell you will need:

- a few drops Dragon's Blood Oil
- a red candle
- charcoal
- brazier
- goggles
- sandalwood powder
- an amethyst stone or crystal small enough to carry with you
- rigging knife

The evening of the full moon and just as it begins to rise take the Dragon's Blood Oil and dress the candle. Dressing a candle means you rub the oil up and down the candle to coat the outside of the candle with a thin layer of the oil. As you do this concentrate on the love, or like, of your life coming into your world. Be careful to not attach a face, name, or persona to the wish. Just send the request out into the aether for love. Once the candle is dressed, light the charcoal in the brazier. You may then either wear your goggles around your neck if you wear other glasses or wear them on your face as they were intended. Sprinkle some sandalwood onto the burning charcoal, light the candle, and say:

> Into the aether I cast my wish.
> Sandalwood burns within this dish.
> Candle flames into the night.
> Through this stone I gain my sight.

Pick up the amethyst and stare at the purple stone, placing your desire for love into every molecule of the crystal. When you have put as much energy into the stone as you feel is necessary, leave the stone in front of the candle and allow the candle to burn out. Once the candle has extinguished, place the amethyst in your purse, wallet, or pocket and carry it with you for two weeks to remind you that you are open to love and being loved.

Using your rigging knife, dig a hole close to the most used door to your home and bury the melted wax. This will give you a residual effect of proximity as you leave the house and return each day.

If you are sincere in your search for love and are open to the aether, you should have a new love within a fortnight.

Second Spell

Love Me Oil is an Anna Riva product and may be found at many occult supply stores or ordered online from Indio Products. If necessary you may substitute Passion or Attraction Oil, also both Anna Riva products. For best results, however, you should use Love Me Oil.

For this spell you will need:

- a red candle
- Love Me Oil
- candleholder
- compass
- goggles
- spike

During the full moon cast a short circle. Once the circle is cast, dress the candle with Love Me Oil and set it in a candleholder. Orient yourself with the compass. To self-orient stand at the southern needle of the compass and face north. Once oriented don your goggles and take up your spike with your left hand since that is the hand that is closest to your heart. Facing north, hold the spike directly out in front of you and say:

> I look toward the earth for the gems found there.
>
> Bring the love meant for me.

Turn clockwise toward the east and say:

> As the sun rises, so shall my love. Bring the love meant for me.

Turn clockwise toward the south and say:

> The fire that burns shall heat my heart and the heart of my true love.
> Bring the love meant for me.

Turn clockwise to the west and say:

> We are born from water and water shall bring my intended.
> Bring the love meant for me.

Finally, turn back to the north and say:

> I have been around the compass and have looked into the aether for my love.
> I am ready. Bring the love meant for me.

You do not need to let the candle burn down. Put out the flame and use it again should you need it. It is already dressed and ready.

You are now receptive to love and those who love. You will become more accepting of attention, conversation, and the person who may be your one true love. As you go through your days and on your journeys, be ever vigilant for love in whatever form that may take. Remain open to all persons and situations that will bring the love meant for you.

Remain open to all persons and situations that will bring the love meant for you.

Spells

Travel

We all travel. Many of us travel a great deal, while others seldom leave their hometowns. Travel is traditionally thought of as an air element in Steampunk Magic. However, it may be situation specific to the mode of travel at the secondary level. As we go through the three ways we travel—by air, by water, or by ground—you will see how each mode connects with a different element.

Travel by Air

Flying is statistically the safest mode of travel there is across the United States or in other countries. The amount of traffic that is in the air at any one time is astronomical. However, accidents do happen and they happen to us when we least expect them. And a plane crash is catastrophic. For travel by air, a spell specifically designed around the air element is essential. The air element, also used for new beginnings, is a perfect way to start the spell.

You will need:

- small brazier
- charcoal
- dried lavender
- small fan
- an avatar: a crystal, charm, or any other item that you identify with, such as a photograph or your talisman from the airship

- map showing your current location and your final destination—hand-drawn is sufficient if you aren't able to find a professional version

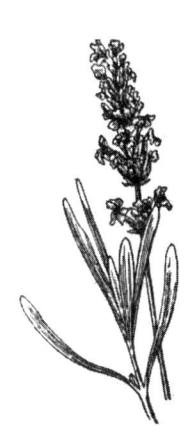

In a quiet place early in the morning, and preferably the morning before you leave on your trip, light the brazier and place a few sprigs of lavender on the burning charcoal. Depending on your capability to tolerate smoke, turn the fan on and point the fan on low toward the brazier. As the sun begins to stream through your window, take your avatar and place it over the map where your departing airport is marked. Think of landing safely at your destination as you move the avatar in a straight line to each airport that you will be visiting during your travels. As you move your avatar, say:

Through time and air from place to place,
Gods insure I reach each safe.

Once your avatar arrives at your destination, leave your hand on it and say:

I have arrived safely.

Spells

For the return journey, repeat the spell the night before you are due to return. As you move your symbol over the individual airports on the map, say again:

Through time and air from place to place,

Gods insure I reach each safe.

When your avatar reaches your home airport, say:

I have returned safely.

You are now ready to travel.

Travel by Sea

Travel by sea is often on vacation. Cruises are becoming a popular short vacation that you can take for a few days or you can book extended journeys to far-reaching destinations. Although cruise ships, cargo ships, and even military ships from the Navy, Marines, or Coast Guard are very safe, there are a number of incidences that always come to mind; Titanic, Lusitania, Andrea Doria, Costa Concordia, Cole, or the Achille Lauro. This spell should keep you safe as you cross oceans.

For this spell you will need:

- a blue candle
- charcoal
- a brazier
- dried comfrey
- live Irish moss

- a dish with about an ounce of water in it
- rigging knife

At sunset of the day before you sail, as the sun is disappearing over the horizon, light the candle. Next, light the charcoal in the brazier, and wait for the coals to heat up. Sprinkle the comfrey over the hot coals. Vision calm waters, bright sun, clear nights, and safe travels as you place the Irish moss in the water dish. Continue to concentrate as you say:

Water deep and water clear,
Travel far and travel near.
Take me out and back again
To where I go and where I began.

Place the Irish moss in a shaded but not dark spot in your house, and let the blue candle burn out.

On the morning you leave for your cruise hold the dish of Irish moss and say:

I leave on this journey in trust and safety.
Let no obstacle bar my way or harm me.
This moss shall bring me back safely.

Place the dish with the Irish moss back in a spot that is protected and not brightly lit.

When you return from your voyage, use your rigging knife to plant the Irish moss in the yard with ample shade and moist conditions. As you fill in the hole around the moss, say:

My safety and protection was aided by this moss
and this moss I shall protect in return.

Travel by Ground

Ground travel is the predominant mode of transportation for most of us. We walk, bike, drive a car or a motorcycle. Some of us ride a skateboard, or perhaps a Segway. Regardless of your mode, you must traverse from point A to point B safely and without incident. This spell will help you whether you are going across town or crosscountry.

If you live in an apartment or condominium then find the closest dirt around the foundation of your building

For this spell you will need:

- 4 Tbsp dirt from your yard

- carrying container—small Tupperware or plastic baggie, to hold the dirt

- a censor with charcoal

- a simple map of where you are going

- Malachite or turquoise stone or a small piece of lead (a fishing weight or lead ball from an antique pistol)

- a few sprigs of lavender

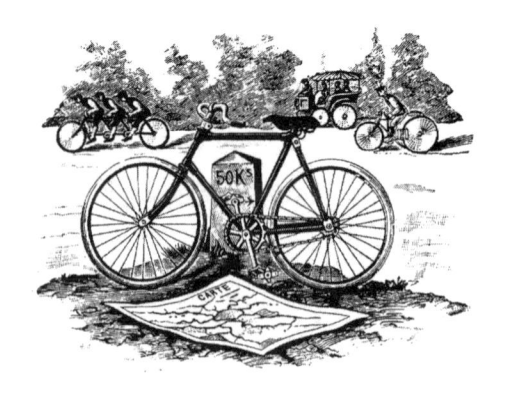

Facing toward your destination place the dirt in the carrying container. Light the charcoal in the censer. As the coals are heating up, lay the map out in front of you and place the stone/lead at your starting point. Place the sprigs of lavender on the burning coal. Holding the dirt container in your dominant hand and the stone/lead in your non-dominant hand. Move the stone on the map from your starting point to your destination and say:

> As I move this stone along its path
> I travel the earth safely and without obstacle.
> May all ways be clear to me for the duration of my travels.

Place your stone or piece of lead into the container of dirt. Then seal the container and pack it along with your map safely for the trip.

When you are ready to return, lay out the map and face the direction of your home. Take half the dirt from the container and scatter it on the ground where you are currently staying. Hold the remainder of the dirt and stone/lead in your dominant hand. With your non-dominant hand, trace your return path home with your index finger, saying:

Regardless of your mode of transportation you must traverse safely and without incident.

> Thank you Earth Mother for allowing me to travel
> here safely and without incident.
>
> Allow me to return home in the same manner.

Then pack the map and remaining dirt and return home.

Once you arrive safely home, scatter the rest of the dirt back where you got it, saving the stone, and say:

I have been safe and successful in my travels due to
your help.
I shall retain your stone in thanks.

Place the stone/lead on your altar for the next time you travel.

Health and Healing

We all want to be in good health. We take vitamins to maintain our health, medicine when we are sick, and undergo invasive operations when there is no other option. When the crew is sick, the ship is sick; therefore, health on an airship is imperative.

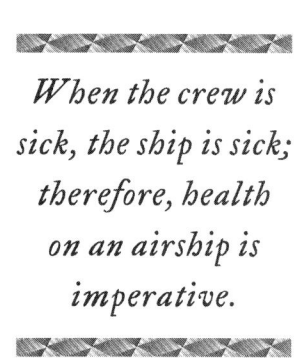

When the crew is sick, the ship is sick; therefore, health on an airship is imperative.

There are two types of spells included in this section; general health and healing. General health is a continuation of a present condition. It is maintaining a successful status and is like preventative medicine. Healing happens when health suffers. Due to our own habits and activities, through an action of others or happenstance, injuries occur. During these times healing is paramount. In the healing ritual we will work at repairing ourselves from the inside out and the outside in.

General Health

If you do not have mint growing in your yard I recommend a garden shop or large building supply store that has a garden section. For a few dollars you can buy a mint plant for your window or yard and be assured of a supply of fresh mint.

For this spell you will need:

- a copper teapot, with water
- fresh mint
- a yellow or orange candle
- a small piece of Jade or Garnet
- rigging knife
- yard

At sunrise heat the water in the teapot and place a few leaves of fresh mint in the hot water. Allow the tea to steep as you prepare the rest of the spell.

Find a spot where the first rays of the rising sun may find you—either outside or in front of an eastern-facing window. As the first rays of light shine on you, light the candle.

Pick up the stone in your left hand (use the left hand because it is the closest hand to your heart, which is the center of your being) and hold it so the sun's rays bathe the stone in light.

Say:

As the sun sustains all things, so shall the sun sustain me.
Charge this stone that I may remain healthy for my journeys.

Drink the mint tea as the candle burns down.

Once the candle has burned out, dig a hole close to your most used door with the rigging knife and bury the melted wax. This will radiate residual health throughout the year.

You should not need to do this spell more than once or twice a year. It is a sort of maintenance spell. If you need health more than that, you should use the healing spell. Also remember that a spell does not replace conventional medicine or medical practitioners. Part of any magical system is to maintain your other routines that are successful, such as having regular medical checkups and following medical advice and directives.

General health is a continuation of a positive present condition.

Healing

The healing spell is similar to the health spell but is more specific. Use this spell if one of your crew is ill or injured.

The holes in holey stones are caused by water eroding through river or ocean rocks. These rocks are powerful talismans that when worn around your neck will promote healing and health. They are used to envision healing in the individual by peering into the outer aether and seeing the cause of the illness, and thusly enabling one to strike down that cause to heal oneself. Holey stones may be purchased, but if you are fortunate enough to find one it will be much more powerful since it was yours from the beginning.

If you prefer to peel or slice the apple before eating it, be sure to use your rigging knife. Even though food preparation is a kitchen duty, magical food preparation is a function of the Steampunk Magical tools and therefore the rigging knife is required.

Note: This spell is not meant to replace professional medical attention, the emergency room, or continual care by a licensed doctor. It is used to augment other medical procedures and attentions.

For this spell you will need:

- fresh spearmint
- lime

- a copper teapot
- a yellow candle
- a holey stone
- apples
- blackberries
- rigging knife
- yard

Just before noon, prepare spearmint tea in the copper teapot. Season with lime and set aside. At noon, in a space with plenty of natural light, light the candle. Hold the holey stone in your left hand and say:

As this stone withstood the erosion of eons to remain
only slightly scathed,
so with this stone bring me back to health.

Eat some of the apple and blackberries and drink a cup of the spearmint tea.

Extinguish the candle while saying:

I shall draw the energy of this candle to heal from within and without.

Repeat this spell for the next six days at noon if possible but at some time during the day. Wear the holey stone around your neck or carry it with you. As with the health spell, bury the remaining candle wax near the most frequently-used door for residual healing energy.

Apples and blackberries are strong healing fruits and should be consumed each morning until healing is accomplished.

Expulsion

We all wish to expel something from our lives: bad habits, people who are around us and just won't go away, feelings we may or may not be able to identify the origin of, or something internal, such as doubt or fear. Many use the term "banishment" for this ritual of getting rid of something that you just can't or won't live with anymore. This spell works as a barrier between yourself and that which you wish to be rid of.

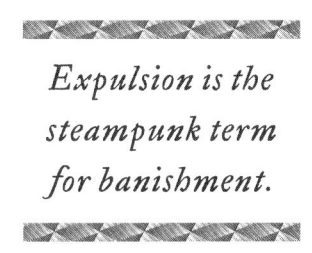

Expulsion is the steampunk term for banishment.

Flight clothing was necessary due to the extreme cold from the altitude that ships fly at. In this spell, you will be working with hot coals, and body coverage is important for safety.

For this spell you will need:

- rigging knife

- heavy brazier (A small fire pit works well, or an old hibachi. Whatever you use, make certain there are handles that won't heat up because you're going to need to pick up the fir pit later on.)

- coal

- goggles

- pumice stone

- compass

- flight gear: heavy leather gloves; long trousers and a long-sleeved shirt, both made of heavy material

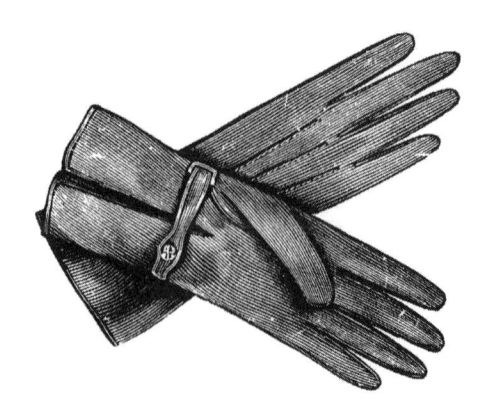

At midnight of a new moon, go to the most northern point of your property. Clear a section on the ground to place the fire pit, making certain there is nothing flammable above you. With your rigging knife, dig a hole approximately a foot deep. Place the coal pieces in the brazier and get the fire red-hot. Don your goggles and take the pumice in your left hand. As you grip the pumice tightly, say:

> I expel (whatever you are trying to get rid of in your life)
> from my present and future.
> I confine all that I expel into this piece of airy stone
> and through fire I cleanse my life of (whatever you are ridding yourself of).

Safely place the piece of pumice on top of the glowing coals. Once the pumice has heated up and begins to glow, carefully lift the brazier and dump the coals and pumice into the hole, saying:

> I bury (whatever you are getting rid of) and am now free of it.

Cover the hole with dirt as you say:

> Be gone from my life and torment me no more.

Tamp down the earth and turn your back on the hole. You have now expelled and banished your fears or other issues to the earth, where they will bother you no more.

Success

I have listed success separately from wealth, since money is not always someone's idea of success and success does not always involve money.

If you wish to carry the marble in this spell as a talisman, find a small chip from a local countertop company. They usually will give the chips away. If you wish to use the marble as the base or altar for the spell then find a larger piece. Again the same companies will usually give the pieces away if you aren't particular about the shape or color. When I went to get a piece of marble for this spell, the lady at the shop that cuts countertops took me to the back of the yard. She said, "If you want to buy a piece we stop now. If you want a piece free then we walk a little more." I opted for the free piece, and we walked another twenty-five feet to a large pile of broken pieces of every color marble you could imagine. I found a lovely piece of black marble and have used it ever since. She was very glad to have helped.

For this spell you will need:

- a piece of marble (see note below)
- a green candle
- an orange
- rigging knife

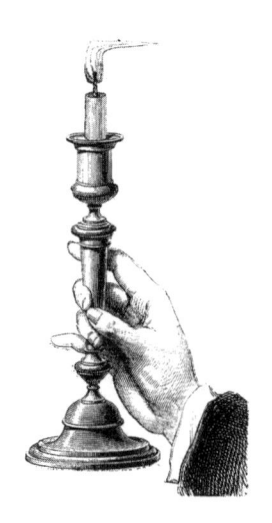

At high noon cut a hole in the top of the orange just large enough for the candle to fit inside upright. Take your finger and dip it into the hole, covering your finger in orange juice. Dress the candle with the juice. If you are using the marble as an altar, place the orange on the marble. If you are using the marble as a talisman, place the piece of marble inside the orange, and then place the candle in the fruit on top of the marble. Light the candle and say:

> The sun heats my air and allows me to travel to where success awaits.
> As this candle burns so shall my success increase.

Once the candle has burned completely, remove the talisman, wipe it off, and carry it with you. If you used an altar-size piece of marble then wipe that off and place it where your wallet, keys, or purse can sit on it.

With your rigging knife, did a hole and bury everything else in the yard close to your front door or whatever door you use most often. This will give you a secondary effect as you pass by the spot on your way to work, sports, entertainment, or whatever else you need success in.

Remember that success does not always mean money.

Wealth

In these hard financial times, wealth is oftentimes not a luxury but a necessity, and wealth is often situational to where you are in life. In this spell wealth means an increase in your personal finances. This spell does not dictate how much or how little you will gain, merely that you should see a noticeable increase to your finances.

Because blackberries need to be pruned on a regular basis, you might be able to find a dried sprig on an older or dried back branch. If you cannot find a pre-dried branch, then thank your deity for the sprig before cutting one. Only cut what you need and do it respectfully.

For this spell you will need:

- a sprig (a three-leaf branch) of blackberry leaves
- a coin from the year you were born
- a vanilla bean
- three small tiger's eyes
- a small sachet or bag
- a few dried thistle leaves
- a piece of charcoal
- a brazier

At the sunrise of the day of the full moon, place the blackberry sprig, coin, vanilla bean, and three tiger's eyes in the sachet. Tie the bag very tight and hold it in both hands. Place the charcoal in the brazier, light it, and sprinkle the thistle leaves over once it's hot. Hold the bag in the smoke of the thistle and say:

Gods and Spirits increase my wealth as you see fit.
As this smoke surrounds this small sachet so shall
wealth surround me.

Then raise the bag above your head, and as the sun's rays strike the bag say:

> Golden energy, fill this bag so that I may reap its bounty.
> My wealth shall increase as you see fit.

Carry the bag with you as you perform your everyday duties as a talisman of wealth. Be ever cognizant of the chances to increase your wealth and be vigilant toward losing the wealth that you have. If you have decisions to make concerning wealth you may use the sachet as an inspirational piece to guide you.

CONCLUSION

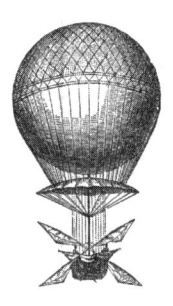

Ships and sails proper for the heavenly air should be fashioned. Then there will also be people, who do not shrink from the vastness of space.

—Johannes Kepler, letter to
Galileo Galilei, 1609

In this book I have given you the basics for a system of magic derived from the steampunk movement so currently popular. It is important to remember that Steampunk Magic is not tied to the popularity or fad of steampunk literature or characters in television or movie plots; the tenets of Steampunk Magic transcend the facets of the genre to stand alone.

This book has given a brief history of the Steampunk movement and how that movement led us to this system we now practice. Anyone can practice Steampunk Magic. There is no secret that only a few are privy to. There is no individual, also, who is precluded from this system by virtue of a religious mandate. Steampunk Magic, therefore, is among a very small and select group of systems that include everyone. And that is one of the benefits of the system.

Since the times of the ancient Greeks, philosophers and rhetoricians have discussed the aether and its effects on humanity as it affects the gods that breathe it. They have supposed its existence, and as the scientific community has grown and philosophies were joined by the cold hard facts of logic and scientific principles, the aether has continued to be studied, explored, and traveled through. At times the theory of the aether has fallen under review as the popularity of particular gods and spirits of our different paths has ebbed and flowed. There are now some who doubt the aether as they doubt the gods that dwell above it. These individuals have accepted other paths and other deities to preclude all others. In their religion there is no place for the aether or those who reside there. In Steampunk Magic we know that the aether exists. We see its effects on a daily basis, and through our spells and rituals we tap into the powers of the aether in our magical day-to-day workings.

I have been as specific as possible with the introductory chapters of this book since the basics are always paramount in any new endeavor. I have given you a detailed explanation of the tools that are unique to the Steampunk Magician, and I have tried not to overlook the altar pieces that are common to most traditions. In the end I think I have done a good job at both; you the reader will make the final review of my successes.

It is important at the end of this that we remember where we came from and where we are going. The rituals and spells will work under a number of situations and using a myriad of tools. Steampunk Magic gives a push to these spells, and many—well, actually all—of these spells are specifically written and practiced in the Steampunk Magical System.

One last thought as you board your airship and fly into the aether: do not be anchored by this book. Use it as your instruction manual to the new ship you have signed on to. Take the maps and charts given in these pages, check your ship's stores for your tools and equipment lists, and fly true. The next chapter of Steampunk Magic is yours to write.

EPILOGUE

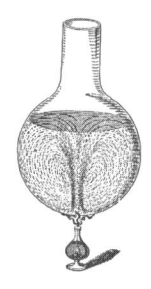

The last couple to arrive is also the last couple to leave the old Victorian house. It is a little after midnight, and they have stayed later than they had anticipated, having another small glass of absinthe with the host. The gentleman, still sporting his pistol and carrying a new copper walking stick, a present from the airship for his work on the ritual that night, held the door for his wife. He would go back to work in the morning teaching history at the local high school. His wife would rise in the morning, and instead of corset and goggles, she would don a three-piece skirt suit and deal with mortgages most of the day behind her desk at the bank.

The rest of the airship, most already home and asleep, would similarly return to their day lives: an engineer, two other teachers, a stay-at-home dad with two preschool children, a factory worker at the local car plant, a couple that drive long haul for a national trucking company and only make it when they are in town, and five students at different colleges and universities in the area. The only member not going to work or school in the morning would be their host. He is retired and will spend the morning cleaning up from the night before and then work in his basement creating something even more interesting for the next month's ritual.

As pagans we are constantly reminded that we are no different from anyone else. So it is too with Steampunk Magicians. Our system is only as different as the tools we use to wield the same energy everyone else does. I would like to think that we do it with panache and a great sense of style. But that's a personal opinion and not always shared with the general public. Therefore, to each his own. See you on the airship next time.

RESOURCES

When Charles Edward Mudie created the first lending library in London he did so as a way to both serve the population of the time and to preserve many authors' works and make them available to the general public. With the creation of Mudie's he also set the stage for the librarian, who until this time worked often as a private consultant, to become the resource that they are today. Below are lists (since librarians are famous for creating them) of some sources you may find helpful in your research. This list is not exhaustive, nor does it attempt to be. I strongly suggest that you add to this list as other books and sites become available in the future.

Books

When K. W. Jeter coined the term "steampunk," I don't think he ever envisioned the popularity of the movement and genre. He and his friends were sitting in a small coffee shop trying to make a living as writers. Now more than thirty years later the steampunk phenomenon has grown to include everything from fashion and retro-technology to role playing games and literature. There are many very good books on the history and culture of steampunk. Here are a few.

Cunningham, Scott. *Cunningham's Encyclopedia of Crystal, Gem and Metal Magic.* Saint Paul, MN: Llewellyn Publications, 1998.

Friesen, Christi. *Steampunk-Style Jewelry: Victorian, Fantasy, and Mechanical Designs, Necklaces, Bracelets, and Earrings.* Minneapolis, MN: Creative Publishing International, 2009.

Gevers, Nick. *Extraordinary Engines: The Definitive Steampunk Anthology.* Nottingham, UK: Solaris Books, 2008.

Gibson, William, and Bruce Sterling. *The Difference Engine.* UK: Gollanz, 1990.

Grymm, Dr., with Barbe Saint John. *1,000 Steampunk Creations: Neo-Victorian Fashion, Gear and Art.* Beverly, MA: Quarry Books, 2011.

Heinlein, Robert. *Stranger in a Strange Land.* New York: Ace Books, 1991.

Hewitt, Jema. *Steampunk Emporium: Creating Fantastical Jewelry, Devices and Oddments from Assorted Cogs, Gears and Other Curios.* Cincinnati, OH: FW Media, 2011.

Jeter, K. W. *Infernal Devices: A Mad Victorian Fantasy.* New York: St. Martin's Press, 1987.

Jeter, K. W. *Morlock Night.* DAW, 1979.

Lloyd, G. E. R. *Aristotle: The Growth and Structure of His Thought.* Cambridge: Cambridge University Press, 1968.

Lynn, Andrea. *Shadow Lovers: The Last Affairs of H. G. Wells.* Boulder, CO: Westview Press, 2001.

Moore, Barbara, and Aly Fell. Steampunk Tarot card deck. Saint Paul, MN: Llewellyn, 2012.

Smith, William. *Dictionary of Greek and Roman Biography and Mythology.* London: Harper & Brothers, 1851.

Strongman, Jay. *Steampunk: The Art of Victorian Futurism.* London, UK: Korero Books, 2011.

VanderMeer, Ann, and Jeff VanderMeer, eds. *Steampunk.* San Francisco, CA : Tachyon, 2008.

VanderMeer, Ann, and Jeff VanderMeer, eds. *Steampunk II: Steampunk Reloaded.* San Francisco, CA : Tachyon, 2010.

VanderMeer, Jeff, with S. J. Chambers. *The Steampunk Bible: An Illustrated Guide to the World of Imaginary Airships, Corsets and Goggles, Mad Scientists, and Strange Literature.* New York: Abrams, 2011.

Westerfeld, Scott, and Keith Thompson. *The Leviathan Trilogy.* New York: Simon & Schuster, 2010–2012.

Teague, Gypsey. *Victoria X: Tales of an Aireship.* Create Space, 2011.

Clothing

Most religions, the pagan movement included, are known for black clothing. Go to a pagan gathering and you'll likely see a plethora of black robes, dresses, cloaks, trousers, and hats. It seems like there is no color in the pagan community at times.

Fortunately, Steampunk Magic does not adhere to the black cloak uniform so often referenced during ritual. Steampunk Magic, and steampunk in general, has a more Victoriana approach to clothing and accouterments.

Clothiers, either individual businesses or large corporations, have a wide variety of steampunk clothing options and there are also costumers who do their own work. In an attempt to assist you in finding the right accessory to your day-to-day steampunk life and magical experience I have added resources below.

Clockwork Couture

www.clockworkcouture.com
A good place to look is Clockwork Couture. Here there are exceptional corsets and other undergarments for the complete Victorian look. You may also find timepieces and hats. This company has a wide assortment of clothing and accessory items for both men and women. They are easy to work with and reasonably priced—especially if you shop their sales page.

Dracula Clothing

www.draculaclothing.com
Don't let the name Dracula throw you off. This is a company with some great Victorian Gothic clothing. They are housed in Prague and deal with euros. I have not ordered anything from these folks yet, but they look interesting.

Hot Topic

www.hottopic.com

Another company that does a small selection of steampunk fashion is the trendy mall store Hot Topic. Their Tripp line of olive drab canvas jackets, gloves, and halter tops are military inspired, with quality construction and that industrial feel that many look for in their costumes. This is the perfect flight gear if you are looking for something to last a long time. I have not seen the line in their catalog for a while, however, I see their discount pieces at their stores often.

Steampunk Emporium

www.steampunkemporium.com

For those who are looking for more traditional and period fashions, there is The Steampunk Emporium. This company is an offshoot of Gentleman's Emporium, sort of a J. Peterman's for the steampunk fan. They have a wide selection of well made men's and women's wear and accessories as well as period pieces such as opera glasses, compasses, and bathing suits. Look for their variety of assortments that they call Brassy Bits.

Pyramid

www.pyramidcollection.com

One of the more trendy companies getting into steampunk fashion is the new age online retailer Pyramid. Pyramid sells all types of clothing, but they recently have started carrying a wider variety of professionally made jackets and skirts directly marketed to steampunk fans.

Conventions

The gathering of like-minded individuals goes back in time to the cave dwellers who created groups for safety against the elements and outside threats. In this day and age there are conventions for every interest and there are new conferences and meetings springing up almost daily. The small sampling of steampunk conventions listed below are those that I am very familiar with but the list is by no means meant to be exhaustive. Please feel free to add to it with what you find to be useful or delete what you find to be of little or no use to you.

Anachrocon

www.anachrocon.com
Anachrocon is a fun conference held in February in the Atlanta area. It is a strictly steampunk conference and they get close to 1,000 people per year. The panels are well organized and informative, and the central bar and restaurant gives everyone a chance to see and be seen throughout the weekend.

*Dragon*Con*

www.dragoncon.org
Dragon*Con is the largest science fiction/fantasy convention in the southeast. With a self-reported attendance of over 40,000, they have something for everyone and a large steampunk instruction and education track. Held Labor Day weekend in Atlanta, the convention takes up seven hotels with overflow to ten others. They also have a parade on Saturday that draws over

150,000 spectators. The steampunk portion of the parade is especially fun to participate in.

Steampunk Exhibition Ball

www.steampunkexhibitionball.com
This is a major steampunk event held in Seattle every January. As the self-claimed, and relatively uncontested, home of United States Steampunk, this ball is a fine example of west coast steampunkerie.

Steampunk World's Fair

www.steampunkworldsfair.com
This is what it claims. A great event in New Jersey in May. This hosts a myriad of makers, performers, artists, and other venders with a wide variety of entertainment.

Upstate Steampunk

www.upstatesteampunk.com
I am very biased toward this conference since I own it. However, other people seem to like the conference very much and come back year after year. This is held in the late fall in the northwest corner of South Carolina and draws around 250 attendees. Upstate Steampunk also has a very active group base in upstate South Carolina that does something almost every month—either dining out at local pubs, or in the warmer months outside at local parks.

Music

I love music. I listen in the shop when I'm working on the latest creation, I listen at work as background noise, and when I write I find inspiration from many of the artists and bands listed below. Every year a new band or artist will appear to catch the attention of the listener, and since steampunk is becoming ever more popular the genre of steampunk music has grown in popularity. Below are a few of my personal favorites. I am certain that you will create a list of your own very soon.

Abney Park

www.abneypark.com
What can you say about Abney Park? They are amazing and have continued to please for quite some time. Whenever I need inspiration in the shop or at home writing, I usually have some Abney Park playing. Their YouTube videos are also quite fun to watch. They have now branched out into a roleplaying game and a novel, so they are diversifying.

The Clockwork Dolls

www.theclockworkdolls.com
I particularly like this band. They currently only have one album out. I heard at Dragon*Con that they have changed band members and they are back in the studio writing and recording another album. I am quite convinced that it will be as good as the first one.

The Clockwork Quartet

www.clockworkquartet.com

These are thirteen young musicians with alter egos that perform as a full steampunk orchestra. No idea why they are called a quartet.

Doctor Steel

www.en.wikipedia.org/wiki/Doctor_Steel

Doctor Steel's albums and live shows set the stage for many of the current steampunk bands. They influenced Diesel Punk, Goths, and the Riverheads.

Frenchie and the Punk

www.thegypsynomads.com/

Up until a few years ago, this duet was called the Gypsy Nomads. Frenchie is an amazing vocalist, and her husband who goes by "the punk" writes and plays almost everything. I have to admit they are one of my favorite bands because they are friends of mine.

The Men That Will Not Be Blamed for Nothing

www.facebook.com/blamedfornothing

This is a London-based band named after graffiti linked to Jack the Ripper at the last crime scene. Historians now believe that the Ripper did not write the line found on a wall near the last body and that it was probably a religious reference to the

London-based Jews. However, that has not prevented the story from getting airplay as well as the band.

Professor Elemental

www.professorelemental.com/fr_home.cfm
Professor Elemental is a hip-hop steampunk musician. With the song "Fighting Trousers," he proves he can use Queensberry Rules successfully while going shirtless in a boxing ring wearing a pith helmet.

Valentine Wolfe

www.valentinewolfe.com
Valentine Wolfe is my favorite steampunk/goth band. Braxton and Sarah are amazing in their range of both voice and instrument abilities. They are a constant pleasure at many steampunk conferences in the southeast and are the house band at Upstate Steampunk.

Tools

I love tools and I love toys, which in my case are often tools. While we make much of what we use in Steampunk Magic and I have tried to give you a start in the tools chapter of this book, there are times when either money or time is applied to something else and you want your tools quickly. At that point you need someone whom you can trust to make your items for a fair price and deliver them to you in a fair amount of time. The craftspeople listed below are some of those people whom I either have personally worked with or have known others who have.

Directional Gear

For those in need of a hand-poured bronze Directional Gear, contact Nathan Smith at the Art Department of Clemson University. Nathan is the artist who designed my airship's directional gear, and we are very happy with it. I am certain that after Nathan graduates from Clemson he will go on to create even greater pieces of art, but the one piece I shall always be thankful for is my directional gear. He may be contacted at *nathansmith256@gmail.com*.

You may also contact Professor David Detrich, Professor of Art, Sculpture at Clemson University at *ddavid@clemson.edu* or (864) 656-3890.

Goggles

Atomefrabrik
An interesting company that does an amazing array of goggles at *www.atomefabrik.com/pages_goggles/steampunk.htm*.

Steampunk Emporium.
They have a good selection of inexpensive goggles at *www.steampunkemporium.com/store/steampunk_goggles.php*.

Upstate Steampunk
The goggles in this book were created by them at their small shop. You may contact them at *www.upstatesteampunk.com*.

Wands

MacFie's Wizard Shop

This company does magical wands for costume play as well as wands for use in circle. Their selection of steampunk wands are interesting. Visit them at *www.macfies.com/steampunk-collection.html.*

Upstate Steampunk

The wands in this book were created by them at their small shop. You may contact them at *www.upstatesteampunk.com.*

INDEX

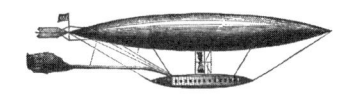

A

Abney Park, 13, 204
absinthe, 68, 71–73, 195
Adjutant, 42–43, 45
Aesthete, 34, 37, 41
aether, 19–24, 30, 48–49, 56, 77, 90, 95, 97–98, 101, 104, 109, 117, 122, 130, 135, 138–142, 147, 150–151, 157, 161, 165, 168–169, 171, 180, 192–193
alternative history, 11, 17
Anna Riva, 169
Antarctic Press, 12
apple, 74, 137, 140, 181–183
Aristotle, 22, 199
Artificer, 39
athame, 53, 76–77

B

Ballew, Braxton, 151, 206
blackberry, 188
boline, 74, *75*
brazier, 87, 134, 145–146, 167–168, 172–175, 184–185, 188

C

cakes and wine, 42, *45*, 48, 68–69, 74, 83, 86, 90
Captain, 28, 38–39. 42–44, *45*, 49, 56, 86, 89–90, 92, 96–97, 100–104
censor, 176
Chaos, 21
comfrey, 174–175

209

Commander, 38–39, 42–44, 45, 49, 56, 97–100, 102–103
Compass, 24, 36, 50–51, 75–76, 83, 89–90, 104–105, 169–171, 184, 201
cyberpunk, 10-11

D
Daedalus, 22
Dawson, Richard, 159
Directional Gear, 49–50, 52–54, 76, 83, 86, 89, 91–92, 94, 97, 103–105, 207
Dove's Blood, 167
Dragon Con, 11, 14–15, 17, 202, 204
Dragon's Blood, 167-168

E
Explorer, 34, 36, 38, 41

F
Fabulae, 21

G
Gaia, 22
Gaius Julius Hyginus, 21
garnet, 179

goggles, 1-2, 5, 13–14, 16, 24, 36, 56–68, 82, 90, 105, 138, 167–170, 184–185, 195, 207
goth, 9–10, 29–30, 200, 205–206

H
hematite, 54, 87, 94, 150
High Priest, 33, 37
High Priestess, 2, 33, 37

I
Icarus, 22
Irish moss, 174–175

J
jade, 179

K
key, 39, 50, 80–81, 81–82, 92–93, 96–97, 103, 134
Kitty Hawk, 22
Klima, John, 11

L
lamp, 24, 36, 77, 91, 97–98, 151
lavender, 172, 176–177
lime, 182
Love Me Oil, 169–170

M
malachite, 176
marble, 185–187
Mess Officer, 41, 43, 45

N
Navigator, 36, 43–45

P
Poe, Edgar Allan, 29–30
pumice, 184–185
Purser, 41–42, 45

R
radian, 75
rigging knife, 74, *75*, 86, 90–91, 105, 112, 122, 158, 162–163, 165, 168, 175, 179, 182, 184, 186

S
salt cellar, 78, 92, 98
sandalwood, 168
Shelley, Mary, 8, 31–32
Shipwright, 40–41, *45*, 85, 97–98, 103
spike, 76–77, 88, 91, 104, 164, 169
Steampunk Exhibition Ball, 11, 203

Steampunk Magazine, 11
Steampunk tarot, 153, 199
Street Urchins, 34

T
tarot, 83, *84*, 93, 153, 160, 199
Tesla, Nikola, 14, 30
tiger's eye, 188
Tinkerers, 34
turquoise, 177

U
Upstate Steampunk, 15, 203, 206, 208, 212

V
Valentine Wolfe, 151, 206
Verne, Jules, 6, 8, 26–30
Victoria, 6–7, 10, 24–25, *25*, 29, 32, 135–136, 138–139, 141

W
wand, 48, 53–55, *55*, 76, 80, 82, 88–89, 91–92, 104–105, 208
Wells, H.G., 6–8, 26–28, 30

ABOUT THE AUTHOR

Gypsey Elaine Teague is the Branch Head of the Gunnin Architecture Library at Clemson University. She has advanced degrees in Business Administration, Landscape Architecture, Regional and City Planning, Library and Information Science, and Community Mental Health Counseling. She is an elder in the Georgian Tradition and the originator of the Steampunk Magical System. She is a noted lecturer and author, with seven novels including *The Arks of the Convenant, Victoria X: Tale of an Aireship,* and *Dragonfly Over New Europa,* as well as seven reference books including *Practical Chainmail in the Current Middle Ages, New Goddess: Transgender Women of the 21st Century,* and *A Social and Psychological Account of Gender Transition: The Diary of a Transsexual Academic.* She presents regularly at library and popular culture conferences on gender and steampunk. With her spouse she is the owner of Upstate Steampunk, a conference for steampunk fans in South Carolina. Visit her online at *www.upstatesteampunk.com.*

TO OUR READERS

Weiser Books, an imprint of Red Wheel/Weiser, publishes books across the entire spectrum of occult, esoteric, speculative, and New Age subjects. Our mission is to publish quality books that will make a difference in people's lives without advocating any one particular path or field of study. We value the integrity, originality, and depth of knowledge of our authors.

Our readers are our most important resource, and we appreciate your input, suggestions, and ideas about what you would like to see published.

Visit our website at *www.redwheelweiser.com* to learn about our upcoming books and free downloads, and be sure to go to *www.redwheelweiser.com/newsletter/* to sign up for newsletters and exclusive offers.

You can also contact us at *info@redwheelweiser.com* or at
Red Wheel/Weiser, LLC
665 Third Street, Suite 400
San Francisco, CA 94107